THE BEST IN TENT CAMPING

MINNESOTA

Other titles in the series:

THE BEST IN TENT CAMPING

A GUIDE FOR CAR CAMPERS WHO HATE RVs, CONCRETE SLABS, AND LOUD PORTABLE STEREOS

MINNESOTA

TOM WATSON

MENASHA RIDGE PRESS
BIRMINGHAM, ALABAMA

Dedicated to Doug "Mr. B" Barkley and the memories of
Boy Scout Troup 22.—Tom Watson

Copyright © 2005 by Tom Watson

All rights reserved

Printed in the United States of America

Published by Menasha Ridge Press

Distributed by the Globe Pequot Press

First edition, first printing

Library of Congress Cataloging in Publication

Watson, Tom, 1947—

    The best in tent camping, Minnesota: a guide for campers who hate RVs, concrete slabs, and loud portable stereos / by Tom Watson.—1st ed.

p.cm.

Includes bibliographical references and index.

    ISBN 0-89732-573-7

    1. Campsites, facilities, etc.—Minnesota—Guidebooks. 2. Camping—Minnesota—Guidebooks.

    3. Minnesota—Guidebooks. I. Title.

GV191.42.M6W38 2005

917.76'068—dc22

2005041657

CIP

Cover and text design by Ian Szymkowiak, Palace Press International, Inc.

Cover photo by Tom Watson

Cartography by Steve Jones

Indexing by Galen Schroeder

Menasha Ridge Press

P.O. Box 43673

Birmingham, Alabama 35243

www.menasharidge.com

TABLE OF CONTENTS

CENTRAL MINNESOTA

SOUTHERN MINNESOTA

APPENDIXES

MINNESOTA MAP KEY

NORTHERN MINNESOTA

CENTRAL MINNESOTA

SOUTHERN MINNESOTA

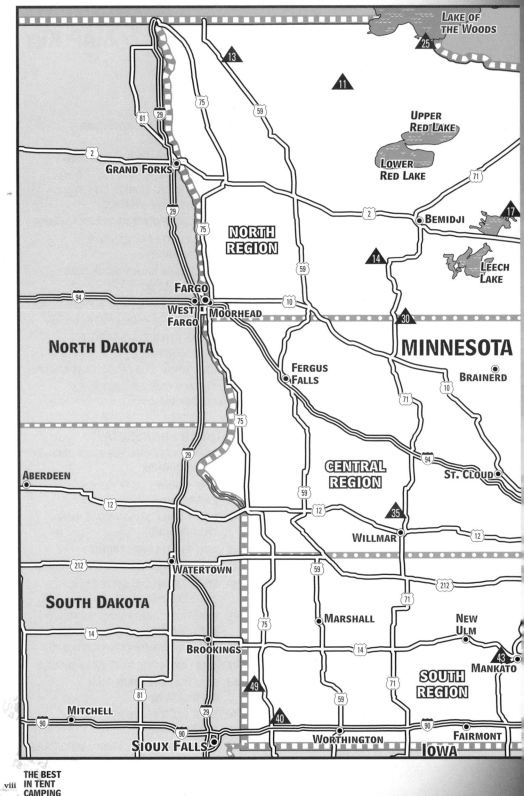

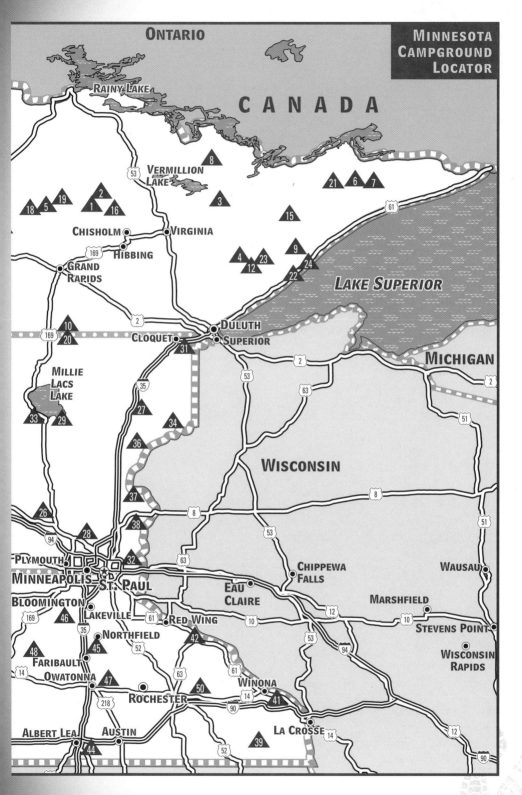

MAP LEGEND

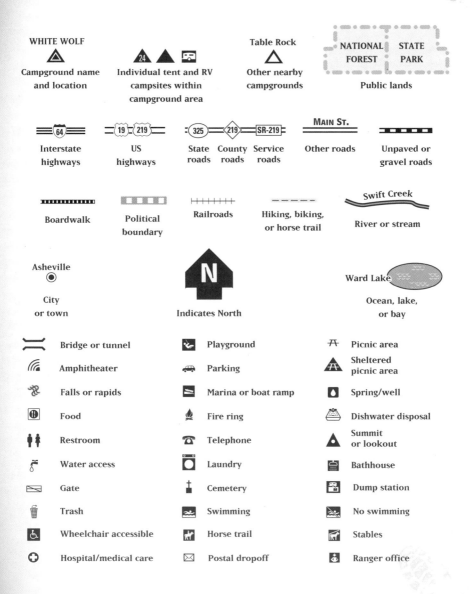

WHITE WOLF

Campground name and location

Individual tent and RV campsites within campground area

Table Rock

Other nearby campgrounds

NATIONAL FOREST | STATE PARK

Public lands

Interstate highways

US highways

State roads | County roads | Service roads

MAIN ST.

Other roads

Unpaved or gravel roads

Boardwalk

Political boundary

Railroads

Hiking, biking, or horse trail

Swift Creek

River or stream

Asheville

City or town

N

Indicates North

Ward Lake

Ocean, lake, or bay

Bridge or tunnel

Amphitheater

Falls or rapids

Food

Restroom

Water access

Gate

Trash

Wheelchair accessible

Hospital/medical care

Playground

Parking

Marina or boat ramp

Fire ring

Telephone

Laundry

Cemetery

Swimming

Horse trail

Postal dropoff

Picnic area

Sheltered picnic area

Spring/well

Dishwater disposal

Summit or lookout

Bathhouse

Dump station

No swimming

Stables

Ranger office

ACKNOWLEDGMENTS

MY DAD PLANTED THE outdoor seeds in me—fishing, hunting, hiking, and camping. By today's standards, our trips were pretty basic, but they instilled in me a lifelong love of the outdoors. I also spent many a great weekend outdoors in Missouri with my Uncle Dick, Aunt Rubelle, and my cousins. There were countless wonderful summer nights in tents or, more likely, the old Ford station wagon, where cousin Bruce and I, along with my younger cousin Robin, would sleep restlessly awaiting dawn and a chance to hit the nearby catfish hole. They were like brothers to me, and their family has always been like a second family to me—and we all loved to camp! Thank you.

Special thanks goes to the person who taught me not only so many skills but the values behind them—my Scoutmaster and friend Doug Barkley. He and the gang in Troop 22 in Minneapolis provided me with some of the best camping memories I shall ever have. The sacrifices made by Mr. B. and other parents to get the troop out camping can never be repaid. Those were wonderful days of rain-soaked Baker tents, rock-hard ground, and dedicated honing of outdoor skills regardless of the weather. We learned more than how to camp—we learned self-reliance and confidence, and we learned to respect the outdoors. For that I shall always be indebted to Mr. B.

Thank you, Lynn, my sister, who is always there to help with such projects, who always has a good idea or an encouraging word. When I wasn't camping out, I was crashing at her place on the way to or from a campsite. Thanks Mom, too!

Last, a big thanks to everyone involved with these campgrounds, from the rangers and staff who keep things together and who share their love and knowledge of these fantastic areas, to the volunteers—the camp hosts who are there to welcome all who come. Thank you all.

PREFACE

ALTHOUGH I CAN'T REMEMBER my very first camping trip, I can certainly remember something from the hundreds since then that I've enjoyed throughout my life. Back then, camping was easy—there were fewer parks from which to choose and fewer conveniences. Every site was a "rustic" site and you didn't expect anything more than a picnic table, a fire ring, and a fairly level patch of ground on which to pitch a tent. It must have left its mark, because even today, with all the options before me, those basic amenities are all that I require and still consider a cushy campsite.

Picking a finite number of camping sites to include in a "best of" listing is not an exact science. Are 25 sites too few, are 100 too many? What's the likelihood one can truly stick to the criteria and actually hit that exact number? What about the 62 best sites or the 43 best? More important, I feel, is that the criteria remain constant and based on unchanging standards that the author can share with the reading audience.

Hopefully, your knowing what I look for in a campsite will help you interpret my selections in this book. I grew up loving the outdoors, the wilder places, the less developed areas. I graduated from Minnesota's College of Forestry and have spent 20 years as an occasional naturalist and outdoor writer. I love camping away from the madding crowd, sometimes off the trail and without a tent. Backpack camping is my first love—drive-up camping is a convenient and comfortable second. Spending a weekend in a big metal box on wheels in the middle of a paved picnic area is not camping in my book—it's blasphemy of the term.

Be advised, some state parks offer fantastic natural amenities but lousy campsites. Some state forests have wonderful campgrounds—the best in the state—but few other amenities. Voyageurs National Park and the Boundary Waters Canoe Area Wilderness are almost exclusively water-access campsites and were not among those considered for this particular book, although both could provide 50 great campsites at the unfolding of a map. Purposely left out, too, were the scores of backcountry campsites available within the Chippewa and Superior National Forests. Most of these are accessible only by water or at the end of long trails. They offer some of the most remote, pristine, and self-reliant camping in the state.

Sadly, there are no private campgrounds listed either. Space is money, and private campgrounds offer very little privacy and tend to either pack 'em in hubcap to trailer hitch or provide sterile, gridwork sites on parking lawns with broomstick trees—hardly what you can call camping.

Still, I must confess, I admire those who at least attempt to enjoy the outdoors at whatever level. It's not so much where you stay while you share in that pleasure, but merely that you do go at all. For those of you, however, who do appreciate the tent pad and fire ring, who seek the quiet, rustic places—or at least a sense of it—this list of 50 great camping sites is for you.

—*Tom Watson*

THE BEST
IN TENT
CAMPING

A GUIDE FOR CAR CAMPERS WHO HATE RVs, CONCRETE SLABS, AND LOUD PORTABLE STEREOS

MINNESOTA

INTRODUCTION

IMAGINE IF IN THIS STATE of 10,000 lakes each of those lakes had a campground beside it? Well, there are actually more than 12,000 bodies of water that qualify for lake status, and a large number of them do indeed have at least one or two campsites nestled about their shorelines. Some of these are accessible only by canoe or other water vessel; some require a lengthy hike over challenging terrain; and some are connected by at least a thread of a roadway. It's those in this last group that are represented in this particular guide as some of the best tent-camping opportunities in Minnesota.

The interesting and alluring thing about Minnesota, besides those lakes, is the diverse geology and natural character of this northern state. One can enjoy camping in three distinct but overlapping regions: the southeastern Big Woods region, accented by remnant hardwood forests lining deep, glacially carved river valleys; the expansive western region with the remains and restored segments of the vast prairies and oak savannahs that once spread across the middle third of our nation; and the awe-inspiring northern boreal forests of majestic pines, aromatic evergreens, and glimmering birches that blanket the rocky outcroppings and islands throughout the northern shore region. These areas are preserved and showcased in literally hundreds of campgrounds scattered throughout Minnesota.

Most of these campgrounds are gems within a state park, state forest, or national forest jewel box. Some are multifaceted campgrounds, whereas others seem more like hidden stones as yet unpolished by the jeweler's wheel.

The fall colors and blufftop vistas from Great River Bluffs State Park south of Winona to the dog hair–thick clusters of paper birch at Zippel Bay State Park on the southern shores of Lake of the Woods are just a few of the wonderful sights awaiting visitors to our state parks. Others, such as Tettegouche, showcase thundering waterfalls and offer isolated campsites that are the very best of the best. Still others are within the seven-county region of the Twin Cities and offer beautiful, rustic sites just off major freeways.

Minnesota's many state forests and two national forests (Chippewa and Superior) offer dense stands of northern conifers and hardwoods amid lakes of all sizes—camping here is a convenience for those who love to hunt and fish in these scattered forest preserves.

Whether you enjoy camping amid the exposed rock shelves of the Canadian Shield at a northern shore campground or amid prairie flowers and the nighttime howl of coyotes in the middle of a western Minnesota grassland, you can be assured that these 50 campsites will provide both the avid and the occasional camper with many summers—and winters—of splendid campsite options.

Each agency offering camping facilities has plenty of information to help you choose and, in some cases, to secure a site in advance. Please refer to the information within each listing and the reference list in the appendix. Whether you head up north, out west, or down south, there are campgrounds awaiting you, no matter what your fancy! Grab your tent and sleeping bag and enjoy!

THE RATING SYSTEM

Included in this book is a rating system for Minnesota's 50 best campgrounds. Each campground has certain attributes that are ranked using a five-star system: beauty, privacy, spaciousness, quietness, security, and cleanliness. Five stars are ideal; one star is acceptable—all are subjective to some extent and dependent on the other campers at any particular time. Each site is rated based on the collective, overall impression it conveyed during the inspection.

/

In this book, beauty refers to the campground itself, not in the natural amenities for which a park might have been designated. What is the overall layout and shape of the campground respective to its surroundings? Those elements of form, shape, and flow that are revealed in the forest, the waters, and the site itself all contribute to this subjective rating. I consider all the components of the rating system to be interconnected. Those components and the level or impact of any external or artificial elements contribute collectively to creating a sense of beauty about a particular site.

PRIVACY

There is visual privacy, and there is audible privacy. A thick screen of alders does little to provide privacy if the voices of neighboring campers permeate your campsite at annoying levels (total silence is ideal, but impractical). The juxtaposition of driveways, depth and thickness of the vegetation between sites, and the distance between sites themselves are all obvious factors affecting privacy.

SPACIOUSNESS

This is straightforward—is there enough room at the site to park your vehicle, move around the picnic table and fire ring, and still have several locations at which to place your tent? How much room do you have before you step into the living fence surrounding your site or trip over the next site's tent line?

QUIET

Here I considered how often the distractions of neighbors (who are either too close or too rowdy), or the drone of vehicles on a nearby highway (or motorboats on lakes) will keep you from enjoying the sound of the babbling brook behind your tent, or a yodeling loon, or just your own inner peace? Sites that are particularly close to entrance roads or major campground intersections should be regarded with suspicion. Quiet and privacy are closely related.

SECURITY

Usually the more remote sites are, the more secure; the more private the site, the more you can rest assured that no one will get too curious. It never hurts to hide valuables whenever you are away from your site. Be discreet with expensive gear, too. Meet the campground host or ranger and find out how often he or she patrols the grounds. Get to know neighboring campers and volunteer to watch each other's sites.

CLEANLINESS

You can't always rely on the campers who came before to respect the surroundings. Attentive staff members who maintain the grounds are a big plus. Typically, the more remote the site, the less maintenance it receives. Sometimes you may have to do a little more than your share, but it all helps. Practice Leave No Trace procedures when possible. Please help keep these campgrounds clean.

HELPFUL HINTS

One of the easiest ways to learn a bit more about a campground after you've made your initial selection is to call and ask questions. Some campsites can be reserved. Different agencies have their own restrictions and price structures. Some campgrounds listed in this book were undergoing major cleanup operations when I visited. Always check with the local ranger. Contact information is included within each listing and in the agency listings in the appendix.

It is important to know that my criteria for a campground sometimes meant that a state park with incredible scenery or natural attractions was not selected because of its mediocre (or sometimes downright ugly and discomforting) campground.

Reservations can make all the difference. I hope you can trust this guide to give you a better-than-average chance at enjoying your camping outing to its fullest. Have a fantastic time out there!

NORTHERN **MINNESOTA**

BEAR LAKE STATE FOREST CAMPGROUND

BEAR LAKE (not to be confused with Bear Head Lake, further north) is one of two campgrounds selected within the George Washington State Forest. Situated in the upper corner of Itasca County, the uplands are forested and covered in the predominant species—red, white, and jack pine; two common evergreens, white spruce and balsam fir; and hardwoods (mostly paper birch and aspen). The lowlands are characterized by marshes and bogs with tamarack and black spruce making up the patches of trees throughout these areas. Northern white cedar, along with elm and ash, also add to the woodsy appeal of these areas.

This campground was developed in the midst of a marshy area—at least that's the impression one gets driving to the campsite. Bear Lake Campground is like a dry, forested oasis amid marshy, reed-lined bogs and other lowland vegetation. Like many other campgrounds in this region, Bear Lake was developed by the Civilian Conservation Corps.

It's a simple campground, laid out like a dog bone along the northern shore of Bear Lake. Most of the sites are spacious throughout the loop, so the deciding factors are privacy and proximity to the lake.

Site 1 is very spacious but completely open—just to the right of the entrance into the campground. It sits in a large triangle formed by the campground road, a private road leading off to cabins along the lake, and the lakeshore itself.

Site 2 is the closest campsite to the lake—very beautiful, a "great site," as my notes proclaim. Nestled in below red pines mixed with spruce, the site itself is fairly open, but if campers turn their back on the road, there is only the lake beyond the shore to enjoy.

Site 3 is also on the lake. Although not as spacious as site 2, it's a keeper as well. Because the road turns

> *At first it appears to be a big picnic area, but on closer inspection this campground offers a tranquil, lakeside camping retreat.*

RATINGS

Beauty: ✿ ✿ ✿ ✿
Privacy: ✿ ✿ ✿
Spaciousness: ✿ ✿ ✿ ✿ ✿
Quiet: ✿ ✿ ✿
Security: ✿ ✿ ✿
Cleanliness: ✿ ✿ ✿ ✿

KEY INFORMATION

ADDRESS: c/o McCarthy Beach State Park
7622 McCarthy Beach Road
Side Lake, MN 55781

OPERATED BY: Managed by McCarthy Beach State Park; see also Minnesota DNR, Division of Forestry (651) 296-6157

INFORMATION: (218) 254-7979

OPEN: Year-round

SITES: 27 rustic campsites

ASSIGNMENT: First come, first served

REGISTRATION: Reservations not available

FACILITIES: Vault toilet, water, and picnic pavilion

PARKING: No specific areas designated for non-tent site parking

FEES: $10 per night

ACTIVITIES: Fishing, swimming, large picnic area

RESTRICTIONS: Pets: Must be kept on leash
Fires: Must be in cleared areas at least 5 feet around and be built less than 3 feet in diameter
Alcohol: Not allowed
Vehicles: No motorized vehicles on any nonmotorized trails or in areas with posted prohibitions
Other: Hunting and firearms only in posted areas; camping possible in undeveloped areas (special rules apply); check information station for seasonal and special restrictions

back in from the lake after site 3, there is quite a bit of distance between this site and site 6 down the road.

Sites 4 and 5 are big; 4 is on the inside of the loop but right as the road turns back more parallel to the lake. Site 5 is a big, open site shaded by a stand of pines. It has a large grassy pad for pitching a tent.

Site 6 is a big open square, very near the water and offers an exposed grassy site for camping. Likewise, site 7 is exposed. Sites 8 through 11 are all grouped near the swimming area and offer minimal privacy at moderately sized campsites—take your pick!

Sites 12 and 13 are along the outside curve of the loop but still close to the lake. At site 14, however, the road turns up into the wooded area and leads into sites that are not luxuriously close to the lake.

Site 15 is tucked onto the loop right where a dumpster and toilet are stationed. Both it and site 16 share this common utility area.

Sites 17 through 19 are average-sized sites offering the standard amenities. They are, at least, just a short walk away from the lake and the swimming area.

Site 20 is a very open site, one you can look through to see down to the lake. It's a fair distance away from another utility hub—vault toilet and water pump.

The remaining sites are staggered along opposite sides of the roadway. Site 26 is back beyond the large grassy area that includes the pavilion right inside the campground entrance. The last site in the campground is 27. It may be the least desirable site in the camp—but at least it's tucked into the woods.

The pavilion area is not for camping—it's designed for day use. One could literally play baseball in one section and yard games in another while a third group enjoyed a picnic on the grounds—and no one would be in each other's way.

Bear Lake, like many of these northern lakes, is loaded with bass, trout, walleye, panfish, and northern pike. A short walk back out through the entrance and down the gravel road to the east leads to the picnic area and boat ramp for Bear Lake. There are several cabins along the lake to the west of the campground. This campground offers several spacious lakeside sites, all in a groomed, picnic ground setting.

MAP

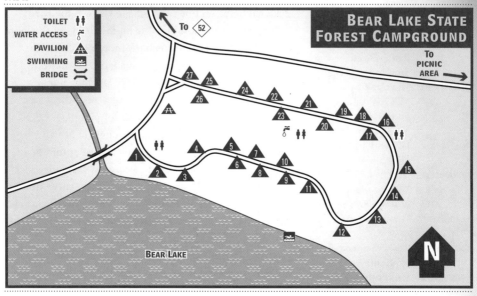

Legend:
- TOILET
- WATER ACCESS
- PAVILION
- SWIMMING
- BRIDGE

BEAR LAKE STATE FOREST CAMPGROUND

To 52

To PICNIC AREA →

BEAR LAKE

N

GETTING THERE

From Nashwauk, take MN 65 north 23 miles to CR 52 (Venning Road). Turn left (west) and go 2.5 miles to the campground entrance on the right.

BEATRICE LAKE CAMPGROUND

> *A rustic, northwoods campground on a peninsular knob that juts out into Beatrice Lake*

BECAUSE **BEATRICE LAKE** Campground is officially an overflow campground for McCarthy Beach State Park, this may seem like a double listing. But because of its rustic atmosphere and distance from the rest of the activities at the "beach," I feel it deserves a place of its own.

Upon leaving McCarthy Park for Beatrice Lake, one of the first memorable scenes one encounters is a boulevard of towering red pines that grow right to the edge of the road. What's more interesting is that the road's lanes are divided by a center boulevard of stately pines, so the roadway becomes a narrow corridor overshadowed by giant, stately trees. The effect doesn't last very long, but the image is reminiscent of Lake Itasca and other "avenue of pines" types of roadways.

Like McCarthy Beach, Beatrice Lake was undergoing extensive site improvements when I visited. In fact, it looked like the cleanup after a tornado when I was there. Still, through all the slag piles and bulldozed berms, there was a homey, woodsy flavor to the sites. There is still a question regarding how many campsites will be retained, removed, or added, so it would be wise to double-check with the park staff at McCarthy Beach before planning a camping trip to Beatrice.

The campsites are laid out along an irregular loop through a mature birch forest dotted with tall red pines and underlain with a solid understory of mixed vegetation. This helps give each site an enclosed, private feeling.

RATINGS

Beauty: ✿ ✿
Privacy: ✿ ✿ ✿
Spaciousness: ✿ ✿ ✿ ✿
Quiet: ✿ ✿ ✿
Security: ✿ ✿ ✿
Cleanliness: ✿ ✿ ✿

Site 1 sits inside the loop right inside the entrance—a basic site with no real features. Sites 2 and 3 are the first of many in which the lake can be seen in the background. Site 2 has trees throughout the site, whereas site 3 is open and spacious. Site 4 is a standard-issue state park site, and 5 and 6 are very exposed sites right across from each other.

Site 7 sits inside the loop away from the lake, while site 8 sits toward the top of a peninsular knob over the lake and offers campers a filtered view through the trees to the waters beyond. Sites 9 and 10 offer a similar background, although site 9 is very close to the road.

Site 11 sits by itself at the top of the hill and therefore probably has the most open view of the lake from the best perspective thus far. Site 12, across the road, is another average site. The next three sites, 13 through 15, are laid out very close to each other—more typical of the bigger state parks. Site 16 is the last site at the end of the peninsula and is perched on a ridge overlooking the lake, too. Site 17 is inside the loop and can be seen fairly easily from neighboring sites.

Sites 18 through 20 are the most remote as they all sit back off the road on a knob of land that juts out to define a small bay at the northern end of the lake. These sites are close enough together that they are not going to feel truly remote, but the fact that they are off the main road means if you have several campers with tents in your party you might be able to secure these three sites as your own group site.

Site 21 captures a bit of this little bay's charm and is one of the most picturesque campsites in this loop. Site 22 overlooks the lake and site 21, but isn't so close as to be overly intrusive.

Of the last eight campsites, only site 25 has any notable view of the lake. The others are stretched around a loop.

This was a simple state forest campground before being turned into an overflow site by the park to the south. I wouldn't let that keep me from checking out this area first as it's more rustic than McCarthy and yet close enough to reap all the benefits of that developed park. Beatrice Lake is a lovely spot with a basic northern beauty, from the rolling hills to the views of the lake through the gleaming white trunks of the paper birch.

Boaters will find the easiest access to the lake is via a public boat ramp just to the west of the campground entrance on CR 52. Both canoers and kayakers will find that the lake's undulating shoreline offers

KEY INFORMATION

ADDRESS:	Beatrice Lake Campground c/o 7622 McCarthy Beach Road Side Lake, MN 55781
OPERATED BY:	Minnesota DNR, Division of Parks and Recreation
INFORMATION:	(218) 254-7979
OPEN:	Year-round
SITES:	32 rustic sites
ASSIGNMENT:	First come, first served, unless reserved
REGISTRATION:	Call (866) 85-PARKS (72757), or online at www.stayatmn parks.com
FACILITIES:	Water, vault toilets
PARKING:	Just past park office and at start of first loop, on left
FEES:	$7 daily permit, $5 group, $25 annual; camping fee $11 rustic; $8.50 nonrefundable reservation fee
ACTIVITIES:	Fishing, boating, all forms of water recreation, hiking, wildlife viewing
RESTRICTIONS:	Pets: On a 6-foot minimum leash Fires: In designated fire rings only Alcohol: Not allowed Vehicles: On designated trails or roads Other: Closed to nonregistered campers 10 p.m.–8 a.m.; use of any type of weapon prohibited; no removal of flora or fauna from park

MAP

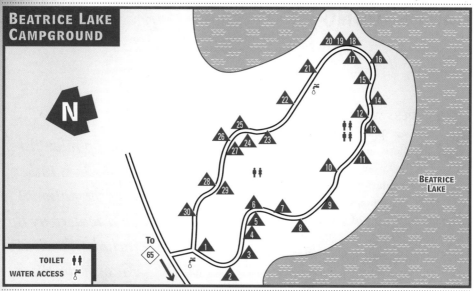

BEATRICE LAKE CAMPGROUND

N

BEATRICE LAKE

| TOILET | 🚹🚺 |
| WATER ACCESS | 🚰 |

To 65

GETTING THERE

From Hibbing, take US 169 North to St. Louis CR 5. Take CR 5 north (left) 15 miles to CR 65. Go left (west) past entrance to McCarthy Beach State Park. Continue north on CR 915 about 3.5 miles past the park to the intersection with Beatrice Lake Road (CR 52). Turn right (east) and go about 1 mile to entrance to Beatrice Lake on right. An alternate route is to stay on CR 5 past CR 65 and continue about 6 miles to CR 52. Turn left (west) and go about 1 mile to campground entrance on left.

myriad opportunities for exploration.

About a half mile outside the entrance to the east, CR 52 intersects with a section of the Taconite State Trail. This trail connects with others within McCarthy Beach State Park to the south, including Snake Trail.

If you don't need additional amenities, you'll find Beatrice Lake overflowing with inviting campsites.

BIRCH LAKE CAMPGROUND

CAMPERS WHO LOVE to fish will enjoy the angling opportunities at Birch Lake. The lake is considered one of the more productive ones in this part of the forest. Its shallow, 25-foot depth and rocky and irregular shoreline provide a perfect habitat for walleye, smallmouth bass, crappie, northern pike, and panfish. The 5,628-acre reservoir is part of a flowage that includes three other lakes.

That being said, it follows that this is a popular lake for motorized fishing boats—currently there are no horsepower restrictions. On a busy fishing weekend, expect to hear the drone of motorized boat traffic throughout the day. Because half the campsites are very near the lake and each has direct access to the water, noise could be a factor during the fishing season.

The area in which the campsite is located is covered in mixed hardwoods. The sites are laid out along two loops, although only half of the northern loop has campsites. The southern loop, laid out in a kidney bean shape, offers a full circle of campsites.

Beginning with site 1 in the northern loop, the surroundings are a bit sparse; the site sits amid older aspen intermixed with red and white pine. It's a basic site with standard amenities. Site 2 sits inside the loop, is small, and is in a stand of scrub poplars. Site 3 is lakeside and sits in a low-lying area. Like site 1, this spot has a direct trail down to the lake. In fact, all the sites on the lakeside are connected to the lake by a pathway leading from each campsite.

Site 4 is one of the closest sites to the lakeshore, while 5, inside the loop again, is set back into the woods. Sites 6 and 7 have a nice overview of the lake, only about 20 yards away at site 6. Sites 8, 9, and 11, all on the inside of the loop, are rather basic, nondescript campsites. The space for your tent is very small and limited at site 10, although it is close to the lake.

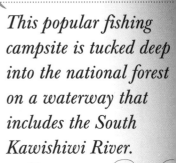

This popular fishing campsite is tucked deep into the national forest on a waterway that includes the South Kawishiwi River.

RATINGS

Beauty: ✿ ✿ ✿
Privacy: ✿ ✿ ✿
Spaciousness: ✿ ✿ ✿
Quiet: ✿ ✿ ✿
Security: ✿ ✿ ✿
Cleanliness: ✿ ✿ ✿

KEY INFORMATION

ADDRESS: c/o Kawishiwi Ranger District 118 South Fourth Avenue E Ely, MN 55731

OPERATED BY: Superior National Forest, managed by Birch Lake Campground concessionaire

INFORMATION: (218) 365-7600; kawishiwi@fs.fed.us; www.fs.fed.us/r9/ superior; campground concessionaire: (218) 365-4966

OPEN: Year-round

SITES: 29 sites

ASSIGNMENT: First come, first served

REGISTRATION: Fee station at entrance to campground; reservations available at (877) 444-6777 or www.reserveusa.com

FACILITIES: Vault toilet, water, dumpster, wheelchair-accessible facilities, boat landing

PARKING: At boat landing

FEES: $12 daily permit, $10 lake sites, $5 for additional vehicle

ACTIVITIES: Fishing, swimming, boating

RESTRICTIONS: Pets: On leash in camp and on trails Fires: In fire rings unless otherwise allowed, such as in backcountry sites Alcohol: Not allowed Vehicles: ATV use restricted to roads and trails Other: 14-day stay limit

The remaining three spots in this area are all cut into old-growth aspen (the typical forest throughout the entire campground). Although site 14 sits on a knoll, this campground's setting is more of a lowland area such as one finds in pockets throughout the north woods—particularly where aspens dominate the forest.

The southern loop features 16 campsites, 9 of which are a short trail section away from the lake. Site 17 is right behind the parking lot for the boat ramp—perhaps convenient but probably noisy with traffic throughout the fishing season. Site 18 is right down on the lake but is very small. Give up space and take the privacy. Site 19 is also nicely located on the lake and was probably designed as an RV site because of its size and the length of its driveway. It's first come, first served here, so if you want this very nice site for your tent-camping pleasure, get here early. I thought it was one of the nicest sites in the whole campground!

By site 20, the road is curving back away from the lake so the rest of the lakeside sites require you walk a bit farther to the shoreline. Site 21 is situated on a rise above the roadway, accessed by a stairway heading up from a turnout parking space along the campground road.

The next few sites are 23 (long and narrow), 24 (too funky, in the undergrowth with hardly any room for a tent), 25 (long driveway but small, gravelly tent space near picnic table), and 26 (featuring a long, narrow driveway through a stand of balsam fir). It, too, has a pathway to the lake.

Vegetation blocks the view into site 27, while site 28 sits back into the woods at the top of a short stairway. Sites 29 through 32 are fairly open, average sites. Of these, only 29 has direct access to the lake. Several of these sites can be reserved: 17 through 21, 23, and 26 through 32.

If fishing is a big part of your camping agenda, Birch Lake—motorboats and all—is probably a good choice. Because of its proximity to Ely and the surrounding backroads laced along and through the Boundary Waters Canoe Area Wilderness (BWCAW), Birch Lake campground is truly a great stopover site to wet a line and warm up with a few canoe strokes in

MAP

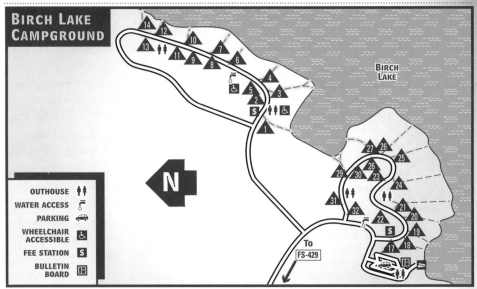

those shallow, rock-bottom bays where the power boaters can't go.

GETTING THERE

From Ely, go south 8 miles on MN 1 to FS 429. Turn right (south) and go 4 miles to the campground's entrance road on the right. The campground is 1 mile down this road.

CADOTTE LAKE CAMPGROUND

> *This modest campsite was cut out of a rough, northern boreal forest and offers lake swimming and fishing.*

CADOTTE LAKE IS ONE of this book's three Superior National Forest campgrounds, all clustered in this old northern boreal forest some 20-plus miles inland from Lake Superior. Like others listed, Cadotte Lake can be looked at as an alternative to the more developed parks that line the north shore of Lake Superior. Also, its proximity to the southern boundaries of the Boundary Waters Canoe Area Wilderness (BWCAW) make this and other campgrounds good lay-over sites when that push from southern Minnesota gets to be a bit too long. Of course, Cadotte Lake offers a quaint retreat, featuring swimming and fishing in a remote, very spacious, private campground.

The camp is laid out in a double loop that parallels Cadotte Lake, giving half the sites direct access to the water. The swimming beach is located just off the boat launching area, and a fishing deck is located a little more than halfway down from loop 1, yet is easily accessible via a trail from the main campground loop road.

There are 12 sites in loop 1, five of which are lakeside with their own pathway down to the shore. All these sites are set into a northern boreal forest consisting mostly of spruce, fir, and aspen in various stages of growth. The dominant understory vegetation is alder, which combines with other understory growth to provide a dense screen between the sites.

Site 2 is a good sample of the campsites at Cadotte Lake: an expanded opening for a campsite at the end of a long, narrow driveway—"keyhole shaped." The sites feature the standard picnic table, tent site, and in-ground fire rings (top rim is flush with ground instead of raised like most rings at other state and federal campgrounds). The long driveway and dense understory make this otherwise very open site quite private.

RATINGS

Beauty: ✿ ✿
Privacy: ✿ ✿ ✿ ✿
Spaciousness: ✿ ✿ ✿ ✿
Quiet: ✿ ✿ ✿
Security: ✿ ✿ ✿
Cleanliness: ✿ ✿ ✿

Site 3 is an open site, and 4 is positioned between the vault toilets and the accessible hydrant—too many utilities too close by for my taste. Like site 3, site 5 has a trail leading down to the lake, as do all the other spots on the lakeside of both loops. Site 8 is a large site off by itself, seemingly private except it appears to be way too close to site 10 (the smallest site in this circle).

Some of these sites have the raised-rim fire rings more common in campgrounds.

Site 11 is the last site on this loop with direct access to the lake (only about 30 yards away). Site 12 completes this loop and is a spacious, open site in a wooded area that appears more natural and less mani-cured than many of the forests in most campgrounds. This is typical of mixed-aged aspen forests—right down to the varying sizes and ages of the balsam fir that are really more understory in this section.

The second loop offers 15 campsites, 5 of which are along the lake. Sites 13 and 14 are long, narrow sites. They back up to site 25, limiting privacy. Site 15 is a long, narrow site that would be very inviting for an RV. Site 16 is a small spot that backs onto site 20 on the lakeside of the loop.

Site 17 is at the end of about a 10-yard trail, setting this camping area off by itself. It's at the end of the sec-ond loop and so enjoys an extra amount of privacy back deep in the woods. Site 18 is another long and narrow site.

A choice site right on the lake is 19. It's a small site with a few boulders and clusters of balsam fir around it (a nice North Shore touch). A short trail along the shoreline to the far end of loop 1 begins at site 19. It's my favorite spot in this campground. Sites 20 through 22 are likewise within this stand of mixed-aged fir.

The following sites can be reserved at Cadotte Lake: 1, 7, 8, 9, 15, 18, 23, and 24. The fishing pier tests anglers' ability to catch northern pike, walleye, and pan-fish. If you're interested in renting a canoe, contact Peter McClelland at (218) 365-4966, and he'll deliver one to your site. Any major services are available in Hoyt Lakes, about 12 miles northwest of the campground.

KEY INFORMATION

ADDRESS: Laurentian Ranger District
318 Forestry Road
Aurora, MN 55705

OPERATED BY: Superior National Forest

INFORMATION: (218) 229-8800; laurentian@fs.fed.us; www.fs.fed.us/r9/superior

OPEN: Mid-May–November

SITES: 28 rustic sites

ASSIGNMENT: First come, first served; some sites reservable

REGISTRATION: Fee station at entrance; reserva-tions at (877) 444-6777 or www.reserve usa.com

FACILITIES: Well, wheelchair-accessible hydrant, toilets, boat launch

PARKING: At boat launch and between campground loops

FEES: $10 lake sites, $8 oth-ers; fee for addi-tional nontowed vehicles

ACTIVITIES: Fishing, swimming, boating, short trail along lake, boat rentals, bait

RESTRICTIONS: Pets: On leash both in camp and on trails
Fires: In rings unless in backcountry sites
Alcohol: Not allowed
Vehicles: ATV use restricted to roads and trails not main-tained for vehicle traffic
Other: 8 person per-site maximum; 14-day stay limit

MAP

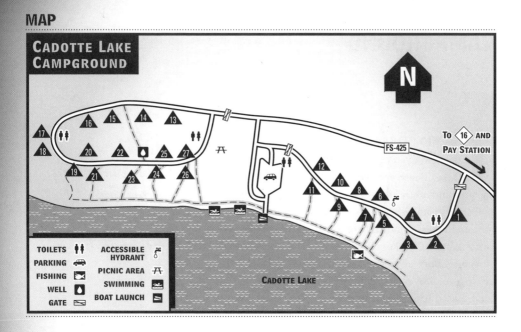

CADOTTE LAKE CAMPGROUND

N

To ⟨16⟩ AND PAY STATION

FS-425

CADOTTE LAKE

TOILETS	♟♟	ACCESSIBLE HYDRANT	
PARKING	🚗	PICNIC AREA	🎋
FISHING		SWIMMING	
WELL		BOAT LAUNCH	
GATE			

GETTING THERE

From Two Harbors, take MN 61 to the intersection with CR 2. Take CR 2 left (north) 13 miles to CR 14. Turn left (west) and drive about 12 miles to Rollins (CR 14 becomes CR 55 at about 10 miles). At Rollins, take CR 44 north (right) about 8 miles to CR 16. Turn left (west) and go about 0.5 miles to FS 425. Turn right onto FS 425 then follow the signs about 1 mile to the entrance to Cadotte Lake campground on the left.

CLUBHOUSE LAKE CAMPGROUND

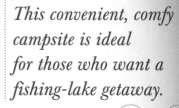

THE BIG ATTRACTION at most of the road access campsites in the Chippewa National Forest is a lake. These are primarily fishing-access camping sites and are used throughout the year as such. This is not surprising when you look at the entire Chippewa National Forest in north-central Minnesota. There are more than 1,300 lakes, 10 percent of the state's bodies of water. Many of those lakes are connected by or are the source of over 900 miles of streams. This is a water-based forest as far as primary recreational opportunities go. While Leech Lake and Lake Winnebigoshish are the two giant waters in this area (not to mention the Mississippi River, streamlike at this stage in its journey to the Gulf of Mexico), there are many more opportunities to find a lake of your own to enjoy.

This convenient, comfy campsite is ideal for those who want a fishing-lake getaway.

What is appealing about Clubhouse Lake is that it is a relatively basic campground—not striking, but suitable for those who enjoy the more rustic setting without a lot of frills and modern conveniences.

Clubhouse Lake campground is laid out in a double loop among red pine trees. This forest is uniformly red pine, both in the canopy overhead as well as the main understory below. The view of the lake through the trees as you drive in sets the mood for this campground.

Site 1 sits within a solid stand of mature and young red pine. It almost looks like a plantation as the trees appear to have been deliberately spaced. Sites 1 through 4 are staggered along the northern loop road that follows the lakeshore. The entire campground is about 50 feet above the lake, but there is direct access to its shores at several points along this road.

Site 5, although fairly open and viewable from the road, is notable for all the birch trees clustered near it These sites all offer a picnic table, fire ring, and tent space. Just before site 6 on the right, there is a trail

RATINGS

Beauty: ✪ ✪
Privacy: ✪ ✪ ✪
Spaciousness:✪ ✪ ✪
Quiet: ✪ ✪ ✪
Security: ✪ ✪ ✪ ✪
Cleanliness: ✪ ✪ ✪

KEY INFORMATION

ADDRESS: Marcell District
Chippewa National
Forest
49554 MN 38
Marcell, MN 56657

OPERATED BY: Chippewa National
Forest

INFORMATION: (218) 832-3161;
www.fs.fed.us/r9/
chippewa

OPEN: May 9–October 15

SITES: 46 rustic sites (suitable for RV or tent)

ASSIGNMENT: First come, first
served; reservations
for 28 sites at (877)
444-6777 or online at
www.reserveusa.com

REGISTRATION: Registration box at
entrance

FACILITIES: Vault toilet, drinking
water

PARKING: No designated areas

FEES: $14 single, $28 double; $9 reservation
fee

ACTIVITIES: Swimming, fishing,
canoeing

RESTRICTIONS: Pets: On leash in
campground
Fires: In designated
rings only; collection
of dead and down
firewood only
Alcohol: Not allowed
Vehicles: ATV use
restricted to forest
roads and trails not
maintained for
vehicle traffic
Other: Quiet time 10
p.m.–8 a.m.; no
firearms or fireworks; reservations
can be made 240
days in advance; 14-day stay limit

intersecting the campground road. This trail extends along behind each campsite in this northern loop and continues down to the lake.

The rest of the campsites in this loop come in a variety of sizes. Sites 7 and 8 are set into the trees on the outside of the loop. Sites 10 through 14 are decent, 14 being an especially long site that might attract RV campers. Sites 18 and 19 are very close to each other and to the intersection with the main entrance road. All 19 campsites in the northern loop can be reserved.

The southern loop sits on a ridge that rises from the lake and main entrance up through the first couple of sites until it levels off at site 23. Site 22 is a long, narrow campsite partway up this ridge. Both it and 23 are in a stand of pines and balsam fir with a few other conifers mixed in. Most of the sites in this loop are pretty average in size and character. Once you start making the turn in the loop to go back toward the lake, the sites become a little more desirable, notably site 32, which is set back into the woods and has ample space. It offers electricity and can be reserved, so expect competition from the RVs again.

Site 34 is rather small and is situated outside the loop as the road turns back toward the lake. All the sites at this end of the lower circle can be reserved. These are the sites that overlook the lake, too. Site 38 is also situated in the big red pines, as are the remaining sites along this loop. One can access the lake via a stairway between sites 41 and 43.

The only amenities at Clubhouse Lake are its clear waters and fishing opportunities.

Clubhouse Lake is also the headwaters for the Bigfork River, where you can launch your canoe as part of the Rice River Canoe Tour, a paddling route through nearby lakes and streams. All in all, this campground rates higher than those at many state parks. So if you are seeking a quiet weekend in this region of Minnesota, it's good to know Clubhouse Lake is there.

The Marcell District of the Chippewa National Forest also offers campers a choice of backcountry camping sites, among the 380 in the forest. These are very remote and rustic with wilderness latrines and fire

MAP

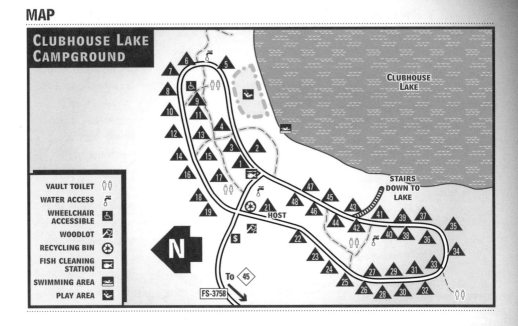

CLUBHOUSE LAKE CAMPGROUND

CLUBHOUSE LAKE

STAIRS DOWN TO LAKE

HOST

To 45

FS-3758

VAULT TOILET
WATER ACCESS
WHEELCHAIR ACCESSIBLE
WOODLOT
RECYCLING BIN
FISH CLEANING STATION
SWIMMING AREA
PLAY AREA

rings. All are accessible via foot or water trails only. Check district national forest offices and information centers for details on this very primitive means of camping.

GETTING THERE

From Marcell, go north on MN 38 for 0.3 miles to CR 45. Go right (east) 5.2 miles to the intersection of FS 2181. Turn left (north) and follow the national forest campground sign 1.5 miles to FS 3758. Turn right (east) and go 1.4 miles to the campground on the right.

CRESCENT LAKE
CAMPGROUND

> *This campground winds along a beautiful, island-speckled lake and has some of the state's best primitive walk-in sites.*

FINALLY, A CAMPGROUND that's not a boiler-plate layout! Instead, it's a crescent-shaped line of campsites that follows the irregular shoreline of the lake and the undulating curves of the topography surrounding it. Here's a campsite that is unique among all those visited. A campground that offers not only spacious drive-up sites, but also five of the more inviting walk-in sites in Minnesota. Yes, I love this campground!

Crescent Lake lies just east of the Sawbill Trail and just outside the boundaries of the Boundary Waters Canoe Area Wilderness. You've got a perfect hideaway here on this 836-acre lake with all its little rocky islands and tall, moss-covered evergreens along the shoreline. It is a motorboat lake, and that is a drawback for purists who don't want to see or hear such mechanization during their camping experience. Still, this is a great spot to play hide-and-*don't*-seek camping with your neighbors.

These campsites are so individual, no two are very much alike until you get right down along the lakeshore—but even then, they retain more individuality than most other campsites in the state. Here's a closer look: there are two camping areas, the stretch along the road paralleling the lake and the units right next to the boat launching area.

The first site along the lake road is 10, a few hundred yards past the road to the boat-launching area. It sits above the long, narrow driveway on a knoll overlooking the road. This is a very private site, nearly isolated from the road and definitely isolated from everything and everyone else in this park. Whereas site 10 is appealing, site 11 is plain, small, ordinary, and close to the road.

Sites 12 through 14 are staggered and cut into the woods either above or below the roadway. They are

RATINGS

Beauty: ✪ ✪ ✪ ✪
Privacy: ✪ ✪ ✪ ✪ ✪
Spaciousness: ✪ ✪ ✪ ✪
Quiet: ✪ ✪ ✪
Security: ✪ ✪ ✪ ✪
Cleanliness: ✪ ✪ ✪ ✪

accessible by short stairways leading from the turnouts for vehicles. Site 15 is a very open site on a level piece of ground. Sites 16 and 17 are both on terraces above the road and each has a stairway leading to the picnic table, fire ring, and tent space that serve as the amenities for this and all sites.

This entire stretch of forest is dominated by fir trees strewn with moss, like tinsel on a Christmas tree—an especially far-north woodsy effect. Sites 16 and 17 sit amid the firs, each situated above the roadway; 17 sits away from the road, too, and is eight or nine steps from it. Site 18 is even farther up off the roadway. It sits on a crest overlooking the lake (a strained view through the trees)—and is at least 15 steps above the parking area next to the road.

There's more of the same at sites 19 (a climb of more than 20 steps to get to this site), 20 situated just above the road, 21, and 22. Pete's Point Trail starts (or finishes) at a trailhead right across the road from the turnout to site 22. This short trail makes its way down to the lake, out to—you guessed it—Pete's Point, and then back again, connecting with the road just past site 17.

Site 23 has a permanent camp "resident" in the form of a giant, four-foot-high boulder situated in the campsite, just beyond the picnic table. Campsite 26 is one of the first sites that is really close to the water. It is laid out along the shoreline. Several small, tree-covered rocky islands are just off-shore beginning at site 26. It and its far-away next-tent-flap neighbor, site 29, are two of the best spots in the drive-up area for grand views of the lake from camp. Sites 27 and 28 sit on the opposite side of the road from the lake and are cut way back into the woods, barely visible from the road.

The last four sites in this section are laid out along the outside edge of a cul-de-sac. Site 30 is a small site sitting right on the edge of the road. These are not very large sites—more typical of sites in other parks. Site 33 did not appear to have a level spot to pitch a tent. Its uneven ground makes it more suitable for an RV rig (did I say that?).

The other section of campground is located next to the boat launch and actually consists of two campsites: drive-up sites 6 through 9 and walk-in sites 1 through 5.

KEY INFORMATION

ADDRESS:	Tofte Ranger District P.O. Box 2157 Tofte, MN 55615
OPERATED BY:	Superior National Forest
INFORMATION:	(218) 663-7280 or www.fs.fed.us/r9/superior
OPEN:	Year-round
SITES:	33 rustic sites including 5 walk-ins; group site
ASSIGNMENT:	First come, first served
REGISTRATION:	Fee station at entrance to campground
FACILITIES:	Vault toilet, water, trash containers, boat access and storage, parking area, barrier-free fishing pier
PARKING:	At boat landing and at pavilion in campground
FEES:	$12 lake sites, $10 other sites
ACTIVITIES:	Fishing, swimming, boating, short hiking trail
RESTRICTIONS:	**Pets:** Must be on a leash and under control in camp and on trails **Fires:** In fire rings unless otherwise allowed, such as in backcountry sites **Alcohol:** Not allowed **Vehicles:** ATV use restricted to roads and trails not maintained for vehicle traffic **Other:** 14-day stay limit

MAP

CRESCENT LAKE CAMPGROUND

TOILET	🚻
WATER ACCESS	🚰
PARKING	🚗
TRASH BIN	🗑
GROUP CAMPSITE	△
BARRIER FREE FISHING PIER	🎣
BOAT ACCESS	⛴
BOAT STORAGE	🛶
FEE STATION	$

CRESCENT LAKE

FS-170

N

GETTING THERE

From Duluth, go north on MN 61 to Tofte. Turn left (north) on CR 2 (Sawbill Trail) and head about 20 miles to FS 170. Go right (east) 7 miles to the campground entrance on the right.

Sites 6 through 8 are right along the edge of the lake, affording a commanding view of the water and beyond—and totally exposed to anyone driving by on this short spur that heads to the boat ramp. These are not sites offering any sense of privacy. Site 9 is at the north end of the spur and separated slightly from site 8. It's next to the trail to the fishing pier and right off a small parking area. Of all the sites in the campground, these are last resorts, in my opinion.

Saving the best for last, I highly recommend the five walk-in sites if you really like to rough it at a very basic campsite. It could get a little muddy along this peninsula after a rain. These five spaced-apart sites are right at the water's edge. The best of these is site 5 at the southern end of a Y-shaped trial spur, about 100 yards from the parking area. It may get noisy at the nearby boat launch, but these are still premium spots for purist campers. This is one of my favorites sites.

DEVIL'S TRACK LAKE CAMPGROUND

I **GUARANTEE THAT** when you drive into the Devil's Track Lake campground you will do a double take on seeing the size of most of the sites here! They are huge expanses of grass. You could arrive in a bus and put up a circus tent and still have room for more. These sites are incredibly spacious—and therefore private.

Being as close as it is to Grand Marais, the lake serves two masters: those who want the amenities of a recreational water playground (motor boating, sailing, and even floatplanes) and those who want to feel that the northwoods is right in the backyard. The campground is laid out on a knobby peninsula at the western end of the lake.

I was dumbfounded when I drove into the site I had selected. The driveway was at least 50 yards long and came to a Y intersection. My site was 4, to the left. That spur went another 40 yards before it came to the campsite itself. By then there was at least 50 yards of dense understory in this thick mixed aspen and balsam fir forest that separated my camp from site 3. A line of trees separated the site from the lake. The rest of the area was a large, lawn-covered field that could easily allow 10 tents ample room. The lone picnic table and fire ring were almost lost in the expansive site.

The campground is basically a long, curving stretch of camping spots along the lake with only four sites on the other side of the road. The road forms a cul-de-sac at the far end and makes a loop with a lone site on it halfway back to the entrance. The area has mostly younger trees—aspen and spruce, the tallest of which are only about 30 feet high. An occasional red pine and a few birch clumps are scattered throughout the woods.

Site 1 is at the end of a 100-foot driveway and opens up into an immense area. The site is off to the

> *The closest campground to Grand Marais, Devil's Track is situated on a peninsula at the western end of a long, narrow lake.*

RATINGS

Beauty: ✿ ✿ ✿
Privacy: ✿ ✿ ✿ ✿ ✿
Spaciousness: ✿ ✿ ✿ ✿ ✿
Quiet: ✿ ✿ ✿ ✿
Security: ✿ ✿ ✿ ✿
Cleanliness: ✿ ✿ ✿

KEY INFORMATION

ADDRESS: Gunflint Ranger
District
P.O. Box 790
Grand Marais, MN
55604

OPERATED BY: Superior National
Forest

INFORMATION: (218) 387-1750 or
www.fs.fed.us/r9/
superior

OPEN: Year-round

SITES: 16 rustic sites

ASSIGNMENT: First come, first
served

REGISTRATION: Fee station at
entrance to
campground

FACILITIES: Vault toilet, water

PARKING: At boat landing

FEES: $14 lake sites, $12
other sites

ACTIVITIES: Fishing, swimming,
boating

RESTRICTIONS: Pets: Must be on a
leash and under con-
trol, both in camp
and on trails
Fires: In fire rings
unless otherwise
allowed, such as in
backcountry sites
Alcohol: Not allowed
Vehicles: ATV use
restricted to roads
and trails not main-
tained for vehicle
traffic
Other: 14-day stay
limit

right of a clearing where campers can get drinking water. Site 2 sits amid a stand of aspen saplings. Sites 3 and 4 are at the end of a long Y-shaped driveway, each at one end of the upper arms of the Y. These are the first sites that sit right on the lake; it's only about 10 feet to the water from these *big* sites! Likewise, site 5 is large, with a long drive drawing you into the trees. Ditto for site 6, which also has young aspens flanking it.

Sites 7 and 8 are at ends of a Y spur, placing each site on a broad plateau—not as big as the others, but very ample and sitting right above the lake's edge. Site 9 is at the end of the driveway that makes a bee-line shot back to the campground. There is what seems to be a pull-through drive off the road at site 10. It's handy because it's blocked at one end; it best serves as a place to park your vehicle so it can at least partially block the view from the road.

Sites 12 and 14 are actually standard-size lots. Site 13 is a small site right on the road. Fortunately there is a small clump of birch serving as a visual screen for this site. The last site at the end of the road before the cul-de-sac is 15, a basic, "small" site when compared to the mega-sites here. Site 16 is off by itself on the back-side of the loop that encircles the entrance.

Devil's Track Lake would be a perfect place for a family that enjoys playing yard games while camping—there's ample room to set up several different games at the same time. Of course the lake is great for canoeing or kayaking. Access to the lake at some sites is down a grassy or earthen embankment with a few boulders. There is a major floatplane base just a half mile down the road from the entrance to the campground. There was no floatplane activity during my brief overnight here, so I can't say how annoying the noise or enjoy-able the activity might be for campers.

Another nice treat about these sites is the open-ness to the sky—this would be an ideal campground for gazing at the Milky Way, summer meteor showers, and the occasional display of the northern lights.

MAP

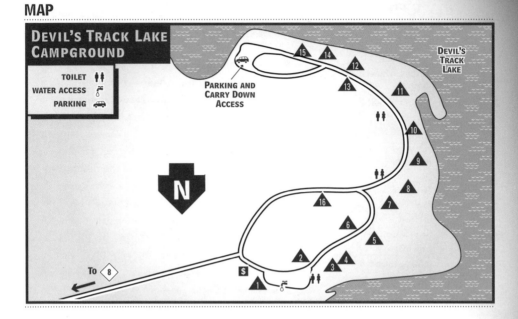

DEVIL'S TRACK LAKE CAMPGROUND

TOILET 🚻
WATER ACCESS 🚰
PARKING 🚗

PARKING AND CARRY DOWN ACCESS

DEVIL'S TRACK LAKE

N

To ⟨8⟩

GETTING THERE

From Grand Marais, take
CR 12 (Gunflint Trail) north
3.7 miles to CR 8. Turn left
(west) on CR 8 and go about
6 miles to the junction with
CR 57. Stay to left and go
about 2 miles to the campground on the left.

FENSKE LAKE
CAMPGROUND

Here you'll find remote camping under an impressive stand of old-growth pines, next to a northern lake and the Echo Trail.

BY THE TIME you've driven into Ely, the spirit of all that is northern Minnesota surrounds you. This is Boundary Waters Canoe Area Wilderness country, whether or not you are actually within its legal boundaries. Up the famous Echo Trail, every turn brings you closer to the remoteness and beauty of this country. Entering the campground at Fenske Lake brings it all home as the road climbs up a ridge guarded by stately white pines with a solid understory of balsam firs and old-growth aspen. As the road continues to the top of the ridge where the campground is located, the forest expands to include jack pines mixed with paper birch.

The campground is an elongated loop of 15 campsites perched on this rise above Fenske Lake. Site 1 is very small and immediately to the left of the driveway into site 2 with its incredibly long, white pine–lined corridor. It sits completely alone on the slopes of this section of the ridge. Its drive-in entrance suggests RV usage.

Site 3 is spacious with an open understory back off the road as well. This campsite is under the cover of mature white and red pine. The campground road is still climbing the ridge at site 4, a nondescript site typical of most campgrounds. Site 5, however, marks the top of the ridge and is a small campsite laid out under this continuing stand of stately pines. Site 6 is a small site—a mini-walk-in with parking off the road and a short (75-foot?) trail leading to what looks to be a picnic site with a tent space at it. Both 5 and 6 are on the outside of the loop and as such are backed by the pine forest. Every site is spread far apart, so privacy is maximized at Fenske Lake—especially at those sites along the backside of the loop away from the lake.

Site 7 is the odd (but beautiful) duck at this campground because it's really a walk-in site situated right

RATINGS

Beauty: ✿ ✿ ✿
Privacy: ✿ ✿ ✿ ✿ ✿
Spaciousness: ✿ ✿ ✿
Quiet: ✿ ✿ ✿
Security: ✿ ✿ ✿ ✿
Cleanliness: ✿ ✿ ✿

on the shore of the lake. There is a pull-out parking space right off the road between sites 6 and 7 (and across from the recycling bins) that marks site 7. The trail drops down through the trees and down the ridge to the water's edge. If you've got the energy to haul your stuff down the ridge and back, this is the site worth staking out.

Site 8 is another "drop-off" campsite—literally. It drops down from the roadway to a level campsite overlooking the lake (through the trees). Site 9 is an inside-the-loop site that sits back from the road. It backs on site 4, but there are plenty of trees and distance to keep this spot secluded as well.

Site 10 sits perched half way between the roadway and the lake, on a plateau on the side of the ridge. Likewise for site 11, except it is slightly more exposed than its neighbor. Sites 12 and 13 have these plateau or shelf sites as well. All look down toward the lake and drop down from the road slightly. These sites offer less privacy than do the sites mentioned earlier. There is a paved access trail to the lake that runs from the parking lot at the pavilion across the road from 13 and winds its way down the ridge (behind site 13). It swings past the picnic area on its way to the fishing pier and beach area on the water.

Speaking of the pavilion, there is another trail behind the shelter that cuts across the loop and then follows behind the campsites along the back loop. It continues around to the lake, crosses site 7, and connects with the trail going from the front of the pavilion to the swimming beach.

Sites 14 and 15 are almost a combination site because they are each on short spurs that come off a Y driveway. Site 14 is the campground host's site; site 15 is right next door—seemingly an arm's length away.

Fenske Lake's group site is noteworthy. It is located back out the main entrance and a few hundred yards farther up the Echo Trail (just past the entrance to the Fenske Lake boat-landing area). This campsite sits atop the ridge, under the canopy of majestic and mature white and red pines. There are two grassy and very spacious areas, both overlooking the lake.

KEY INFORMATION

ADDRESS: c/o Kawishiwi Ranger District 118 South Fourth Avenue East Ely, MN 55731

OPERATED BY: Superior National Forest

INFORMATION: (218) 365-7600; kawishiwi@fs.fed.us; www.fs.fed.us/r9/superior

OPEN: Mid-May– September 30

SITES: 15; 1 group site (3 trailer sites, 7 tent pads)

ASSIGNMENT: First come, first served

REGISTRATION: Fee station at entrance; reservations at (877) 444-6777; www.reserve usa.com

FACILITIES: Vault toilet, water, dumpster, pavilion, wheelchair-accessible facilities

PARKING: At boat landing and at pavilion

FEES: $12 lake sites, $10 others

ACTIVITIES: Fishing, swimming, boating

RESTRICTIONS: Pets: On leash and under control, both in camp and on trails
Fires: In rings unless otherwise allowed, such as in backcountry sites
Alcohol: Not allowed
Vehicles: ATVs restricted to roads and trails not maintained for vehicle traffic
Other: 14-day stay limit

MAP

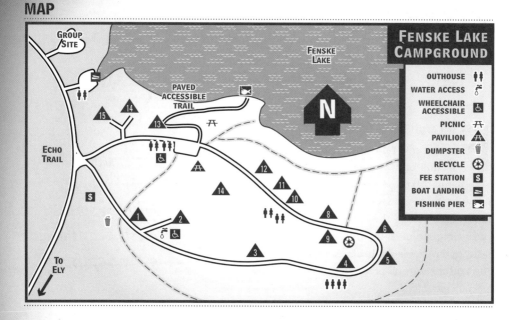

GETTING THERE

From Ely, go 1 mile east on MN 169 to CR 88. Turn left (north) and go 2 miles to Echo Trail (CR 116). Turn right (north) and go 7 miles to the campground entrance on the right.

Fenske Lake looks the part of a BWCAW lake: it's got the rocky, boulder-strewn shoreline and the islands and outcroppings of the exposed Canadian Shield bedrock, and it's been graced with a full forest, including a lush canopy of red and white pines. Campgrounds closer to Ely or those at BWCAW access points may get crowded during the summer. Fenske Lake and other forest campgrounds can provide the perfect alternative for your camping outing. It's also the perfect lake to perhaps avoid the BWCAW area for a weekend of canoeing or fishing.

FINLAND STATE FOREST CAMPGROUND

FINLAND **S**TATE **F**OREST Campground is one of several camping sites clustered in this section of Minnesota's state forest bearing the same name. All these campgrounds offer a basic alternative to the more developed and heavily used state parks nearby along the North Shore. As in other state forest campgrounds, the offerings are modest and basic, and provide few frills. Yet the scenery at these sites and the natural amenities nearby give them a special character.

In the case of Finland's campsites, the fact that the wild and swift Baptism River flows along its western boundary sets this area apart, especially among those who fish for trout. Looking more like a rain-swollen creek than a northern forest river, the Baptism flows behind several of the campsites in this campground. On a still night, with quiet campers, you may hear the sound of these waters rushing through the thick balsam-fir forest.

One key factor in selecting state forest campgrounds should be their proximity to other sites and attractions. In the case of Finland, it sits right off MN 1, which leads to Ely and beyond. There are several other points along this road that are worthy of day trips to backcountry trout streams and lakes. Being only 6 miles from Tettegouche State Park, one of my favorites (see page 75), Finland serves as a handy overflow campground or as an alternative to the more developed and bigger, more popular Tettegouche.

The sites are laid out along a kidney bean–shaped loop. There is a second spur loop of campsites as well as a separate cluster of campsites down the road toward the river. The campsites are nestled into a mixed forest of paper birch and balsam fir. Site 1 is long and narrow, off by itself at the beginning of the winding looped campsite road. Sites 2 through 4 are

> *The rustic sites are tucked into the northern spruce and fir forests near the banks of the Baptism River.*

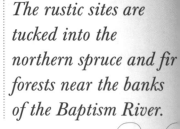

RATINGS

Beauty: ☆ ☆ ☆
Privacy: ☆ ☆ ☆ ☆
Spaciousness: ☆ ☆
Quiet: ☆ ☆ ☆
Security: ☆ ☆ ☆
Cleanliness: ☆ ☆ ☆ ☆

ADDRESS: c/o Tettegouche State Park 5702 MN 61 East Silver Bay, MN 55614

OPERATED BY: Managed by Tettegouche State Park; see also: Minnesota DNR, Division of Forestry (651) 296-6157

INFORMATION: (218) 226-6365

OPEN: Year-round

SITES: 39 rustic sites

ASSIGNMENT: First come, first served

REGISTRATION: No reservations available

FACILITIES: Vault toilets, water

PARKING: At Baptism River cul-de-sac; otherwise only at each campsite

FEES: $10 per night

ACTIVITIES: Trout fishing on Baptism River

RESTRICTIONS: Pets: Must be kept on leash
Fires: Must be in cleared areas at least 5 feet around and built less than 3 feet in diameter
Alcohol: Not allowed
Vehicles: No motorized vehicles on any nonmotorized trails or in posted areas that prohibit use
Other: Hunting and firearms only in posted areas; camping possible in undeveloped areas (special rules apply); check information station for seasonal and special restrictions

appointed with the basics: picnic table, fire ring, and tent site—standard fare through the state.

Site 5 is quite small, barely enough room for one tent. This and other sites are very clean. The dense understory and the distance between sites earn this campground high marks in privacy.

Sites 7 and 8 are the best for enjoying the river because it flows directly behind these two spots that sit outside the western edge of the campground road loop. The road climbs as it snakes its way up to 9, the wheelchair-accessible site. This slightly higher ground gives root to spruce trees and older birch. The terrain is hilly and the road serpentine as it winds through a continually dense forested area.

Sites 10 and 11 are right off the road, but there is ample space between them. Site 12 is a small, open site and the second accessibility site in the loop. As in most campgrounds, this specially marked site can be used by any camper if all other sites are taken.

Sites 13 and 14 are backdropped by a rocky ledge that is exposed at these two sites. The sloped rock face drops right down behind 14. Site 15, across the road from this rocky ledge, is set far back off the road at the end of a cut deep into the woods. There is a real north-woods feel about this site due to the density of the forest in this area. It is definitely one of the most private spots in the campground.

Site 16, located outside the loop, is not particularly notable but offers more of the privacy that is characteristic of this campground. Sites 17 and 18 are open spots laid out in a clearing cut out of a stand of larger spruce. These sites are open and spacious.

At site 17, a spur off the main campground road leads to a side loop with another 10 campsites. These are all basic sites, closer to the state highway and otherwise nondescript.

Continuing along the main campground road, you find sites 19 and 20, which are exposed and close to the road. Site 20 is very well groomed but has an especially small area in which to pitch a tent. Sites 21 and 22 are both open sites—acceptable. Site 23 sits off the road to the left, whereas site 24 is on the connecting road between the main campground route and the

MAP

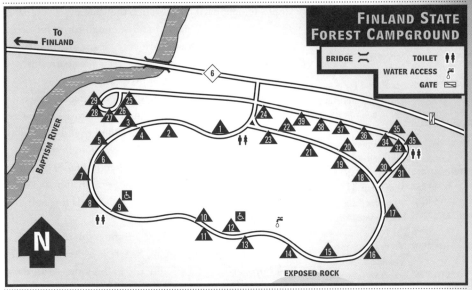

FINLAND STATE FOREST CAMPGROUND

BRIDGE ≍   TOILET ♀♂
WATER ACCESS
GATE ▱

To FINLAND ←

BAPTISM RIVER

EXPOSED ROCK

N

spur loop road. It sits off by itself just inside the entrance to the campground, even closer to the entrance than site 1.

Based on the site layout and the usage I observed, the spur road that heads down to the river attracts the RVs once they enter the park. The road immediately off to the right, parallel to CR 6, heads straight through the woods to an open parking area where sites 26 through 29 form a semicircle around the outer edge of this cul-de-sac. The river rushes past only a few yards away from an open area that would accommodate several RV units. These sites would all look like they belonged together as a group site were it not for the individual signs defining each as separate.

The exception to this cluster of sites is 25. It's off to the left of the area, a long and narrow site cut back into the woods from the open parking area. It's not the prettiest site in this campground but it is separated from the commotion caused by the cluster of sites in the open.

GETTING THERE

From the Ilgen City intersection, take MN 1 north about 6 miles to Finland. Turn right (east) on CR 6 and go about 0.5 miles to the campground entrance on the right.

HAY LAKE STATE FOREST CAMPGROUND

> *This is a perfect retreat for spacious, private camping on a small lake.*

SOMETIMES YOU HAVE to concede that a campsite is just that—a campsite, with no major amenities to speak of, no great natural features to gawk at, and no nearby attractions to head off to for an afternoon romp. Sometimes you just want to find a place to relax, to enjoy the basics—in the peace and quiet of your own spacious campsite. That's what's in store for campers stopping off at Hay Lake.

Granted, there is a lake, and that is clearly enough for most people—especially out-of-staters who don't have the same opportunities to play in the 12,000-plus waterholes Minnesotans enjoy. So from that perspective, Hay Lake fits the bill. Besides the serenity of the lake, there is fishing, boating, and even some undeveloped trail hiking. For birders, and especially for those who enjoy the fall colors, Hay Lake again comes through. As I check the map again, I see it's really not that far from Savannah Portage State Park (about a 40-minute drive to the south) where more lakes and trails abound (see the write-up for Savannah Portage elsewhere in this section).

The campground is laid out in two loops on the southeastern tip of Hay Lake. Although none of the sites is right on the water, several have the lake in the background (viewed through the trees).

As you enter the campground, site 1 sits off by itself on the right side of the road. These are typical northwoods campsites replete with picnic table, fire ring, and tent site. Though this site is not right on the lake, it is located next to a set of stairs leading from the roadway on the first loop down to the lake.

Immediately beyond this access point to Hay Lake is site 2, set in a stand of oaks and aspen. A good distance farther down the road and off to the left is the entrance to site 3—a small, open site compared to the others. All three sites have a thin understory but are far

RATINGS

Beauty: ✿ ✿
Privacy: ✿ ✿ ✿ ✿
Spaciousness: ✿ ✿ ✿ ✿
Quiet: ✿ ✿ ✿ ✿
Security: ✿ ✿ ✿
Cleanliness: ✿ ✿ ✿ ✿

enough apart to afford campers better than average privacy.

Site 4 is an average site, small compared to the long, narrow camping area at site 5. These spots are also situated in that thin understory that is characteristic of this part of the loop. Site 6 is a big, open site with room for several tents. These can be classified as my family group campsites because several members of the same group can share a site without feeling crowded. Site 7 sits so close to the road that it provides no privacy at all.

The second loop has been laid out in a forest stand dominated by maples and northern oaks. Sites 8 through 13 are more open than the sites in the first loop but are more spacious as well. Again, because they are staggered along opposite sides of the roadway these sites don't get in each other's way.

Site 14 sites on a knoll and is backed by a denser stand of woods. You can't see the lake from here, but just before this site on the same side of the road is a small parking turnout at the head of a trail that leads off into the woods toward the lake. Time and rain prevented me from exploring too far along this trail, but I would chance it to say that it probably leads at least to Hay Lake and points beyond.

The next three sites are an odd bunch. Site 15 would be considered a small site even at a state park where such sites are more common; site 16 is right in the open on the outside of the curve of the second loop; and site 17 is a big site but offers no trees for shade or screening—and therefore no privacy. Site 18 shares the dimensions of Site 15 and therefore the honor of being the other "very small" site in this campground.

All is not lost on this second loop, however, as site 20 is off by itself under a moderate stand of balsam, oaks, and maple. It's on the outside of the loop as that roadway becomes the main road leading into and out of the campsite.

The thing that inspired me to keep Hay Lake as one of the 50 best places to camp in Minnesota is that it is remote, not on any main or even secondary roadway, yet it offers a typically northern environment in

KEY INFORMATION

ADDRESS:	55626 Lake Place McGregor, MN 55760
OPERATED BY:	Managed by Savannah Portage State Park; see also: Minnesota DNR, Division of Forestry (651) 296-6157
INFORMATION:	(218) 426-3271
OPEN:	Year-round
SITES:	20 rustic sites
ASSIGNMENT:	First come, first served
REGISTRATION:	No reservations available
FACILITIES:	Vault toilets, water
PARKING:	Small parking turnout at trailhead between sites 12 and 13
FEES:	$10 per night
ACTIVITIES:	Swimming, fishing, hiking
RESTRICTIONS:	**Pets:** Must be kept on leash **Fires:** Must be in cleared areas at least 5 feet around and built less than 3 feet in diameter **Alcohol:** Not allowed **Vehicles:** No motorized vehicles on any nonmotorized trails or in posted areas that prohibit use **Other:** Hunting and firearms only in posted areas; camping possible in undeveloped areas (special rules apply); check information station for seasonal and special restrictions

MAP

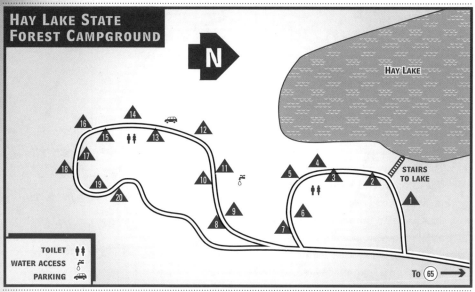

HAY LAKE STATE FOREST CAMPGROUND

N

HAY LAKE

STAIRS TO LAKE

TOILET
WATER ACCESS
PARKING

To 65 →

GETTING THERE

From McGregor, take MN 65 north 26 miles to Ball Bluff. Go about 1 mile farther to the sign for Hay Lake (the turnoff is 2.5 miles south of Jacobson). Turn right (east) and go 3 miles, then turn right (south) and go 1 mile to the campground entrance.

From Grand Rapids, take US 2 east 18 miles to MN 65 at Swan River. Turn right (south) onto MN 65 and go about 6.5 miles to Jacobson. Go 2.5 miles on MN 65 and take the road on the left (east) 3 miles, the right (south) 1 mile to the campground entrance.

which to camp. Maybe it's not the best place for a week's retreat in the woods, but for an overnight stay on the way to somewhere else or as a stop at a small, uncrowded northern lake, it's better than many.

HAYES LAKE
STATE PARK
CAMPGROUND

HAYES **L**AKE **IS ONE** of very few places to
camp in the extreme northwestern corner of
Minnesota. It's not even on many pass-
through routes—you have to want to come here! That
said, this campground would be a typical site in the
more heavily used areas of the state. In this region,
with the Canadian border peeking out at the northern
horizon, it's a quaint, homey campsite in a pleasant
classic northern Minnesota setting.

Situated on a man-made lake created when the
north fork of the Roseau River was dammed, Hayes
Lake is surrounded by hundreds of square miles of
Minnesota "wilderness" protected in the Beltrami
Island State Forest. The park is noted for its scenery
and solitude—the former being especially welcome in
this sparse, flat area. The prehistoric glacial Lake
Agassiz played a major role in shaping this landscape.
The flat topography, with its poor drainage, created
numerous bogs throughout the low-lying areas.
Muskegs created healthy environments for a variety of
wildlife. For a family seeking a chance encounter with
a bear, moose, fisher, otter, bobcat, lynx, and timber
wolf, Hayes Lake is the site to place your bets.

This area was homesteaded in the early 1900s. The
Homestead Trail offers 10 interpretive stops that provide glimpses into the region's historic, natural, and cultural past, introducing visitors to the lifestyle of the
Hendershot family and helping visitors understand
what these rugged homesteaders enjoyed—or endured—
as they struggled to make a life in this desolate region.
The remains of the homesteader building, their worka-
day machinery, and even their gravesites all combine to
offer a telling, personal story about these early settlers.

The main campground is located halfway through
the park, on the northern side of the lake. Thirty-five
campsites are laid along two elongated loops. Each site

> *This isolated camping
> hideaway on a lake
> and stream is tucked
> in the middle of a
> state forest.*

RATINGS

Beauty: ☆ ☆
Privacy: ☆ ☆ ☆
Spaciousness: ☆ ☆ ☆
Quiet: ☆ ☆ ☆
Security: ☆ ☆ ☆
Cleanliness: ☆ ☆ ☆ ☆

ADDRESS: 48990 County Road 4
Roseau, MN 56751

OPERATED BY: Minnesota DNR,
Division of Parks
and Recreation

INFORMATION: (218) 425-7504

OPEN: Year-round

SITES: 35 semimodern
campsites; 1 group
site

ASSIGNMENT: First come, first
served, unless
reserved

REGISTRATION: Available at (866)
85-PARKS (72757), or
reserve online at
www.stayatmn
parks.com

FACILITIES: Restrooms, showers,
vault toilets, water,
trailer sanitation
station

FEES: $7 daily permit, $5
group, $25 annual;
camping fee: $15
semimodern, $18
electric hookup, $11
rustic; $8.50 nonre-
fundable reservation
fee

ACTIVITIES: Swimming beach,
boating, fishing, hik-
ing and nature trials

RESTRICTIONS: Pets: On a leash no
longer than 6 feet
Fires: In designated
fire rings only
Alcohol: Not allowed
Vehicles: On desig-
nated trails or roads
only
Other: Closed to
nonregistered
campers 10 p.m.–
8 a.m.; use of any
weapons prohibited;
no removal of flora
or fauna from park

has its drive-in parking area, picnic table, tent site, and fire ring. The first loop (loop A) contains 26 sites with scrubby understory and grass, resulting in little privacy. Sites are rather close together for my liking but are typical of most DNR sites. The campsites are staggered and not that far from the lake. Sites 22 and 23 are the ones I'd head for first.

Loop B features sites 27 through 35, all of which are surrounded by a stand of young tamarack and spruce. These sites tend to be long, narrow, and cov-ered with grass. Both loops are close to another fea-tured attraction at Hayes Lake—the Bog Walk.

The Bog Walk links up about one-eighth of a mile from the end of the campsite loops. It is fully accessible to people of all abilities. Insect repellent and a bug screen are recommended on the wooden walkway that winds through a wetlands bog area. As a nature trail, the Bog Walk excels. Orchids and other unique bog plants can be observed right from the walkway. Board walkers can birdwatch and view wildlife or just enjoy sitting on one of the many benches along this interpretive trail. The entire wet-lands, from the serpentine shoreline of Hayes Lake to the many creeks of the Little Roseau River, creates a finite ecosystem of special value—especially in these far reaches of Minnesota.

If you are really seeking a hideaway from even the remoteness of the main campground, consider the group camp. It's down a long, sandy, single-lane road through literally miles of jack pine forest. It's not on the lake, but the Pine Ridge Trail does loop through the campsite and can lead campers to the lake as it winds along the forested area north of the lake's lower half.

The Pine Ridge Trail follows the entire canpground side of the lake, and several side loop trails head off from this main trail to create a network of trails throughout the park.

The park borders on sections of the Red Lake Indian Reservation, and there are numerous private properties as well, so it's important and respectful to stay on the designated trails.

For the family wanting a remote, far northern-country experience, far from the madding—or any—

MAP

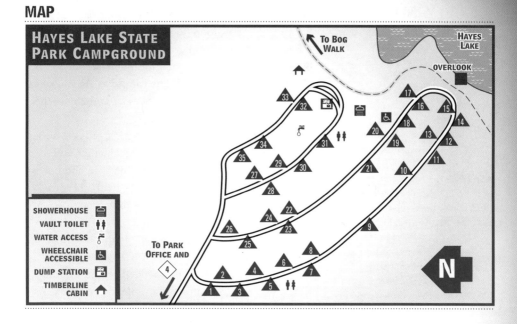

HAYES LAKE STATE PARK CAMPGROUND

To Bog Walk

HAYES LAKE

OVERLOOK

SHOWERHOUSE	
VAULT TOILET	
WATER ACCESS	
WHEELCHAIR ACCESSIBLE	
DUMP STATION	
TIMBERLINE CABIN	

To Park Office and 4

N

crowd, Hayes Lake may be perfect. For the loner or small group of campers, Hayes Lake may be the answer to the quest for solitude.

GETTING THERE

From Roseau, take SR 89 south about 14 miles through Wannaska to CR 4. Turn left (east) on CR 4 and go almost 9 miles to the park entrance on the right.

INDIAN LAKE STATE FOREST CAMPGROUND

> *Roomy campsites situated beneath red pines offer access to a small, northern lake.*

INDIAN LAKE features two campground loops, both close to the lake and each with fairly large, open campsites that offer plenty of room to spread out and enjoy the scattered forest of red and white pines, spruce, and aspen.

Loop B has 18 campsites along a spur off the road leading to the boat ramp. Sites 1 and 2 are large, grassy areas separated by a row of caragana hedging planted as a natural fence between the sites. These are long sites with plenty of room for tents—but probably snatched up by RVs because of the long driveways. The same can be said about sites 3 through 6, too. Site 7 has a view of the lake beyond its boundaries. Otherwise it is typical of the remaining sites within this loop.

There are two trails leading off to the beach area from the main road in loop B. These are located across the road from the access driveways to sites 6 and 8.

Site 11 has a sweetness to it. It's back in a corner by itself—creating a private retreat away from the rest in the loop. Sites 12 and 13 are off toward the water, but both were nondescript, basic sites. Site 14 (part of the loop again) and 15 are both open sites with no privacy from the road. Site 16 was not particularly noteworthy, and 17 is the wheelchair accessibile site. All these sites at the bottom of loop A were very close to the road—not too appealing.

The second loop at Indian Lake features sites labeled walk-ins merely because you have to park your vehicle at a turnout and walk down to them—maybe 20 or 30 yards, tops! This long jaunt through the forest will reward you with expansive sites (in view of each other—the only downside to them) under tall red pines and amid full-bodied spruce trees.

In this same loop are two drive-up sites, 19 and 20. These are in a stand of red and white pine—almost a plantation planting—the red pine aligned to form a

RATINGS

Beauty: ✿ ✿ ✿ ✿
Privacy: ✿ ✿ ✿
Spaciousness: ✿ ✿ ✿ ✿
Quiet: ✿ ✿ ✿ ✿
Security: ✿ ✿ ✿ ✿
Cleanliness: ✿ ✿ ✿ ✿

corridor as you enter this loop. This area is nicely laid out with alders and dogwoods creating a lush understory. The loop is laid out along a ridge or rise above the lake. Site 19 features a tent pad on a flat area above the lake (in the distance). Site 20 is slightly smaller, backed by the woods and very private—except for the fact that it is right across from 19.

Sites 21 through 25 are the walk-in sites. Sites 21 and 22 are off into the woods toward the lake. Site 22 is more open and grassy and a bit farther from the road. Site 23 is a very short distance from the turnout parking area, while 24 has a true walk-in feel to it. Once back in the camping areas, however, sites open up to reveal themselves to each other. Campers in any of these sites can look through a sparse planting of smaller trees to see each other's site—limited privacy from each other, even though they are quite private from the campground loop road. This may not be a bad thing if larger groups—a family reunion or gathering—want to camp together but still maintain some privacy immediately around their own tent site.

Site 25 is open and very spacious but, again, open to a view of the other sites. These sites are further screened by balsam fir throughout the site, so there are some visual buffers throughout this otherwise open area.

All in all, these walk-in sites are large, spacious, grassy areas in which to enjoy this modest lake. One will carry gear 100 feet or less, and there is ample parking for small groups sharing a site or two.

There is a trail along the lakeshore, accessible from all the sites in loop B. There is also a trail leading from site 23 to the water pump and then on to the beach area.

Indian Lake is a shallow lake on the Cloquet River canoe route, making this a great stopover campground or put-in/take-out spot on a weekend paddling adventure. In any case, camping at Indian Lake offers the basics in northwoods settings with a typical—clean, spacious—state forest campground experience.

MAP

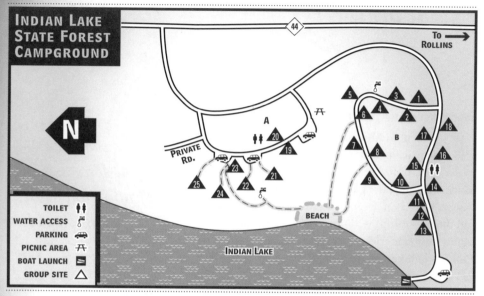

INDIAN LAKE STATE FOREST CAMPGROUND

44

TO ROLLINS →

N

PRIVATE RD.

A

B

BEACH

INDIAN LAKE

Legend:
- TOILET
- WATER ACCESS
- PARKING
- PICNIC AREA
- BOAT LAUNCH
- GROUP SITE

GETTING THERE

From Two Harbors, take CR 2 north 13 miles to CR 14. Turn left (west) and go 12 miles to Rollins, turn right (north) onto CR 44 and drive 1.25 miles to the campground entrance on the left.

ITASCA STATE PARK CAMPGROUND

THERE ARE TWO THINGS every elementary student in Minnesota knows by heart: their state is the land of 10,000 lakes and Lake Itasca is the birthplace of the mighty Mississippi River. Naturally, the park bearing that name attracts tourists who come to enjoy her natural attractions— and often to camp. With more than 32,000 acres within its boundaries, scores of lakes, and more than 50 miles of hiking trails, Lake Itasca pleases all visitors with ease. All that and more waits under majestic northern red-pine forests.

There is nothing more tranquil than boating on a Minnesota lake at sunset. The long, narrow arms of Itasca offer miles of canoeing opportunities. You can paddle from the North Arm boat ramp a thousand yards farther north and come to a small creek flowing gently out of the lake. Pass through the boulders across this flow and keep heading downstream. Well over thousand miles later, you'll be paddling in the Gulf of Mexico!

Launch from that same boat ramp and head in the opposite direction and you'll reach the end of East Arm, where the grandness of Douglas Lodge looms overhead. Step ashore and you are in the heart of the most developed part of this large park. From here you can take several main trails to lakes and points south or you can hop in a car (or on a bike) and enjoy 10 miles of pure northern Minnesota near-wilderness as you wind along the perimeter of the Itasca Wilderness Sanctuary Scientific and Natural Area.

I point out these fabulous natural and cultural amenities early on for a reason: I don't find Lake Itasca to be the greatest place to tent camp! I should explain that as a student at the University of Minnesota's College of Forestry back in the late 1960s, I spent five weeks at Lake Itasca during a field

> *This showcase, pine-forested park features the source of the Mississippi River.*

RATINGS

Beauty: ✿ ✿ ✿ ✿
Privacy: ✿ ✿ ✿
Spaciousness: ✿ ✿
Quiet: ✿ ✿
Security: ✿ ✿ ✿ ✿
Cleanliness: ✿ ✿ ✿

ADDRESS: 36750 Main Park
Drive
Park Rapids, MN
56470-9702

OPERATED BY: Minnesota DNR,
Division of Parks
and Recreation

INFORMATION: (218) 266-2100

OPEN: Year-round

SITES: 237 campsites at 2
campgrounds; 99
electric, 11 cart-in

ASSIGNMENT: First come, first
served, unless
reserved

REGISTRATION: Available at (866)
85-PARKS (72757), or
reserve online at
www.stayatmn
parks.com

FACILITIES: Restrooms, showers,
vault toilets, water,
trailer sanitation
station

FEES: $7 daily permit, $5
group, $25 annual;
camping fee $15
semimodern, $18
electric hookup, $11
rustic; $8.50 nonre-
fundable reserve fee

ACTIVITIES: Fishing, swimming,
canoe and boat
rentals, biking

RESTRICTIONS: Pets: On 6-foot
maximum leash
Fires: In designated
rings only
Alcohol: Not allowed
Vehicles: On desig-
nated trails or roads
Other: Closed to
nonregistered
campers 10 p.m.–8
a.m.; use of weapons
prohibited; no
removal of flora or
fauna from park

semester. We saw the campgrounds every day during that late summer session. They were always full, and the tents were all concentrated into two rather confined areas in this expansive park. I've camped there a few times since my college days, and when I went back there again to inspect the grounds for this chapter, I found that, compared to other sites, even those in other state parks, the campgrounds at Itasca are still pretty average.

The sites are cozy, set under stands of pine or the more common aspen, especially at the Pine Ridge site. They are basic DNR campsites: driveway, picnic table, and fire ring. Bear Paw is at least near the lake, but it is also the preferred site for the big RV units. Pine Ridge is within modest walking distance to the lake and a strip of amenities along the shore, from boat ramp to swimming beach to amphitheater.

Camping at Itasca is convenient for enjoying all the other natural amenities of this park. You probably aren't going to spend a lot of time sitting around your tent—there's too much to do and too many places to see on foot or with wheels of one type or another.

So, here's something only someone reading this book would know: only 8 miles south is one of the most pleasant (albeit basic) tent-camping sites in the state. I am talking about Hungry Man Campground in the northeastern corner of Two Inlets State Forest. It's going to cost you $10 per night to camp there, and there are only 14 sites. The campsites sit on a pine-covered rise above Hungry Man Lake.

Sites 6 through 10 at Two Inlets are the closest to the lake, but all the sites are large with ample room and vegetation, affording privacy. Like most other state forest campgrounds, there are few amenities. Water and vault toilets are the only services. Each campsite has a fire ring and a picnic table. Sites are located both inside and outside the loop with only two sites facing each other.

This is a popular fishing and hunting campground, so it will be busy based on those seasonal activities.

Because it's only about a 10- or 12-minute ride from the campground to the southern entrance to Lake

MAP

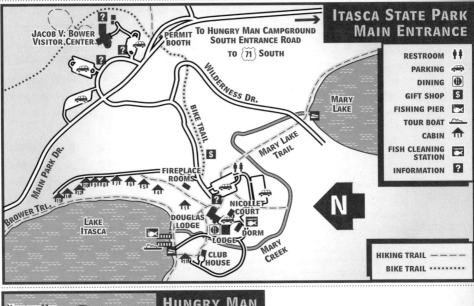

ITASCA STATE PARK MAIN ENTRANCE

Jacob V. Bower Visitor Center

Permit Booth

To Hungry Man Campground
South Entrance Road
To 71 South

Wilderness Dr.

Bike Trail

Mary Lake

Mary Lake Trail

Main Park Dr.

Fireplace Rooms

Brower Trl.

Lake Itasca

Nicollet Court

Douglas Lodge

Dorm

Lodge

Club House

Mary Creek

RESTROOM	
PARKING	
DINING	
GIFT SHOP	
FISHING PIER	
TOUR BOAT	
CABIN	
FISH CLEANING STATION	
INFORMATION	

N

HIKING TRAIL – – – –
BIKE TRAIL ·········

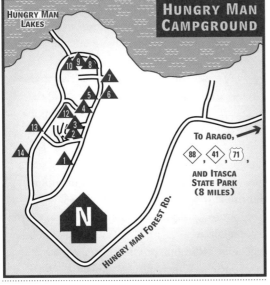

HUNGRY MAN CAMPGROUND

Hungry Man Lakes

To Arago,
88, 41, 71,
AND ITASCA STATE PARK
(8 MILES)

Hungry Man Forest Rd.

N

GETTING THERE

To find the Two Inlets State campground, head south on US 71 until you get to CR 41 at Arago. Turn right (heading west) to CR 88 (on the Hubbard–Becker county line). Turn right (north) to Hungryman Forest Road. Turn left again (west) and go about 0.5 miles to the campground road on your right. It'll be worth the extra time.

Itasca, Two Inlets offers a refreshing alternative to camping in the state park.

LAKE BRONSON STATE PARK CAMPGROUND

> *A dam on the South Branch of the Two Rivers has created an oasis of natural and cultural history in extreme northwestern Minnesota.*

LYING ONLY A COUPLE dozen miles from both the Manitoba and North Dakota borders, Lake Bronson has to be one of the most removed, most isolated state parks in Minnesota's system. Too bad—this park has lots to offer because it sits as an oasis in the middle of this great flat, treeless expanse. Lake Bronson owes its existence to events that happened about 8,000 years ago when a grand glacial lake, Lake Agazziz, began to recede. As it retreated, a series of gravel shorelines were formed. These ridges affected the drainage of streams meandering from the area. When a stream encountered one of these gravel ridges, rapids in the stream or notches cut through a ridgeline formed resistance. In the case of Lake Bronson, that notch was dammed to form the body of water that is today the center of much natural history and outdoor activity: Lake Bronson State Park.

That said, there is one other notable feature about this park. It is situated right on a line that delineates the western prairie grasslands from the more central band of aspen forests in Minnesota. The lake and this significant transitional region combine to form an ideal habitat for a variety of Minnesota wildlife, including the imposing moose. The park is also a haven for deer, an occasional black bear on a trail, over 200 species of birds, 53 mammals, and 24 species of reptiles and amphibians—a variety of fauna that earn this park high ratings for wildlife viewing.

The building of the dam on the south branch of the Two Rivers has been a significant factor influencing the economy and lifestyle of the area, too. In a region with very few lakes, drinking water was always at a premium. Now the lake provides an ongoing water supply and is the main recreational attraction for the entire area, offering the works—fishing, boating, and swimming.

RATINGS

Beauty: ✿ ✿ ✿
Privacy: ✿ ✿ ✿
Spaciousness: ✿ ✿
Quiet: ✿ ✿
Security: ✿ ✿ ✿
Cleanliness: ✿ ✿ ✿

The first thing I noticed when I entered this park was the whiteness on the bark of the aspen trees. Being a forestry graduate, I tend to notice these things right away. I was struck by the fact that they appeared to be paper birch from a distance—their brilliant white bark color deceived me. The park also feature's Minnesota's largest jack pine tree.

Of the two campgrounds in the park, the Two Rivers campground is the one to consider for tent camping. The other campground—Lakeside—is RV central. The individual spaces seemed tight and didn't offer much privacy. Access to this campground is via the park's road, which cuts through the entire developed section of the park, allowing visitors a chance to check out where all the amenities are located. You will pass by a few private properties scattered throughout the park. They seem out of place at first but are hardly noticeable, and not intrusive. Fortunately, some of the park's highlighted features are on the 14-mile hiking trail system that leads off from the end of the road beyond Two Rivers campground.

The campground is rather spacious, but this is somewhat defeated by the fact that driveways into each site are directly opposite each other, reducing the privacy a bit because of that open visual corridor. All the sites are large and sit under big, mature aspens. A sense of spaciousness prevails at each individual site. There is only a modest understory, so privacy between sites is compromised slightly in that regard.

The first loop of campsites, 74 through 128, is a long one; as is usually the case, the best sites are those on the outside head of the loop (104, 105, 107).

The second loop is a smaller version of the first with a few pleasant differences. First there is a thick, woodsy aspen understory in the shadow of a few bur oak trees. These oaks are like an island in a sea of aspen. Some of the sites are long and narrow, others exceptionally broad.

The last loop contains sites 167 through 193, which are laid out in an area that is a transition between the wooded area of the campsite and the savannah grasslands.

ADDRESS: P.O. Box 9 Lake Bronson, MN 56734

OPERATED BY: Minnesota DNR, Division of Parks and Recreation

INFORMATION: (218) 754-2200

OPEN: Year-round

SITES: 194 semimodern sites; 3 hike-in sites; 2 canoe-in sites

ASSIGNMENT: First come, first served, unless reserved

REGISTRATION: Available at (866) 85-PARKS (72757), or online at www.stay atmnparks.com

FACILITIES: Flush toilets, dump station, restroom, showers, water

PARKING: At Lakeside only, along campsites in first loop

FEES: $7 daily permit, $5 group, $25 annual; camping fee $15 semimodern, $18 electric hookup, $11 rustic; $8.50 nonrefundable reservation fee

ACTIVITIES: Picnic area, swimming, boating

RESTRICTIONS: Pets: On 6-foot maximum leash Fires: In designated rings only Alcohol: Not allowed Vehicles: On designated trails or roads Other: Closed to nonregistered campers 10 p.m.–8 a.m.; use of weapons prohibited; no removal of flora or fauna from park

MAP

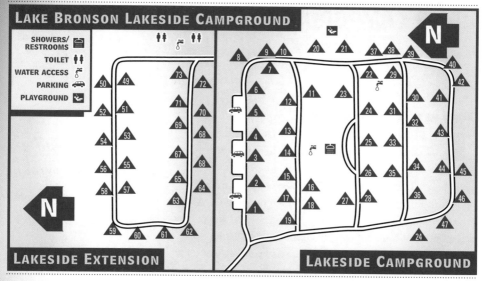

GETTING THERE

Go about 47 miles north of Thief River Falls on US 59 to Lake Bronson. Go right (east) 2 miles on CR 28 to the park entrance on the right.

Because of the topography and amenities, this campground is very similar to the campsites in the southwestern part of Minnesota.

MAP

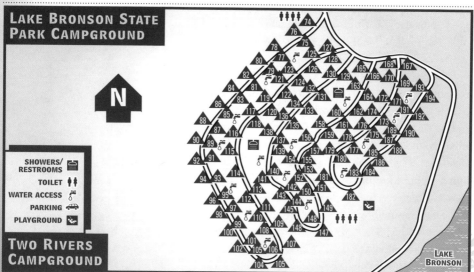

LITTLE ISABELLA RIVER CAMPGROUND

Finland

THERE ARE EXPANSIVE campgrounds and there are small, quaint, out-of-the-way places that you can blink and miss. Little Isabella River campground is one you won't want to pass by! Sure it's small (only 11 sites) and yes, there are not very many facilities or amenities. What it does have is an aura. An aura of tranquility, of relaxation. I think people who drive here not knowing what to expect either leave because there seems to be "nothing" or stay because that "nothing" is really a truly relaxing setting, unencumbered even by overwhelming displays of nature.

Little Isabella River could be the campground where you catch up on the reading you've been neglecting or perhaps hone your sketching skills. If you are a fly-fishing fan, you might simply come here to try to ease a few brookies out of this narrow, shallow, clear-running river.

The simple campsites are laid out along two small loops. This is a forest of mature white and red pines. Although there is some understory, the skyward-reaching trunks are visible through an uncluttered and usually open understory. Each campsite offers the basics of table, fire ring, and tent space—again, the most basic of the basics for Little Isabella.

Site 1 on the east loop sits facing a burned-over area and is not the prettiest site in this campground. Give it a year to revitalize itself with lush, new growth and you'll have to look hard to find any traces of blackened ground. Site 2 sits very close to the Little Isabella River—in all its 10-foot width, shallow depth, and clear-running glory! But the river remains a fast-running course of water that is stocked with feisty brook trout.

Site 3 is small, with a very narrow entrance right off the roadway. Site 4, the last one in this small loop, is a spacious site at the base of those dominating pines. These four sites are completely different from each

> *This very small and modest campground is humbly situated in a stand of pine trees.*

RATINGS

Beauty: ☆ ☆ ☆
Privacy: ☆ ☆ ☆
Spaciousness: ☆ ☆
Quiet: ☆ ☆ ☆ ☆
Security: ☆ ☆ ☆
Cleanliness: ☆ ☆ ☆

KEY INFORMATION

ADDRESS: Gunflint Ranger District 2020 West MN 61 Grand Marais, MN 55604

OPERATED BY: Superior National Forest

INFORMATION: (218) 387-1750; kawishiwi@fs.fed.us; www.fs.fed.us/r9/superior

OPEN: Year-round

SITES: 11 rustic sites

ASSIGNMENT: First come, first served

REGISTRATION: Fee station at entrance to campground

FACILITIES: Vault toilet, water

PARKING: At picnic area

FEES: $10 daily permit

ACTIVITIES: Fishing

RESTRICTIONS: Pets: Must be on leash and under control, both in camp and on trails Fires: In fire rings unless otherwise allowed, such as in backcountry sites Alcohol: Not allowed Vehicles: ATV use restricted to roads and trails not maintained for vehicle traffic Other: 14-day stay limit

other in size, shape, and appeal—very diverse sites, indeed.

Site 5 is the first site on the western loop and sits beneath a mix of towering red and white pines. (The red pines have the "red," scaly bark; white pines have a smoother, greener bark. The needles of the white pine are also finer.) This site has a developing understory composed mostly of young red pine trees. Site 6 has a similar setting but is more open, with an understory that includes other evergreens as well.

I don't have any notes or recollection about site 7; it must be a modest site. Site 8, however, is big and open, still surrounded by those impressive reds and whites. This site sits right above the river and, like all others, it has a well-worn footpath leading to the water a few steps away.

Site 9 is close to the road on a bank above the river. Next to 10, however, it appears to be a big site. Site 10 is noticeably small and otherwise nondescript.

My favorite site here is 11. It's at the end of the west loop; its only neighbor is the tiny site 10 and the river courses behind of the campsite with just a gurgling to hint of its presence. Sitting at the picnic table and looking out past the road, one sees towering pine columns that split the sunlight long before it reaches the forest floor. It's peaceful and pleasant.

Again, this is a campground for people to relax in, chill out, and take in the simple pleasures of Superior National Forest. If you always wanted to work on that northwoods novel, this is a great place to start making notes. Trout fishers usually don't need much more encouragement than a clear, flowing stream and a promise that there are stocked brook trout waiting.

This campground is about halfway between Ely and the North Shore Drive. Other than Birch Lake to the west (see separate listing), there aren't any preferred campgrounds in the entire area except for a few right on the North Shore, on either side of Illgen City. That makes the Little Isabella River campsite a worthy destination when that push to Ely gets to be a bit too long or the North Shore is just a little too crowded. Treat Little Isabella as an overflow option or as the tiny gem of a relaxing retreat that it truly is.

MAP

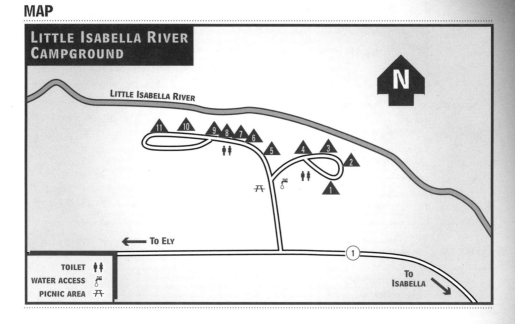

LITTLE ISABELLA RIVER CAMPGROUND

LITTLE ISABELLA RIVER

N

11 10 9 8 7 6 5 4 3 2 1

← TO ELY

1

TO ISABELLA

TOILET
WATER ACCESS
PICNIC AREA

From Duluth go north along the lake to Tofte. In Tofte, take CR 2 (Sawbill Trail) to the left about 25 miles to the campground entrance.

From MN 61 at Illgen City, turn left (north) on MN 1 and go about 16 miles to Isabella. From Isabella, continue 4.5 miles north on MN 1 to the campground entrance on the right.

McCARTHY BEACH STATE PARK CAMPGROUND

> *This long, clear-water, northwoods beach has extensive trails through a pine forest and features rather unusual campsite landscaping.*

IN ALL FAIRNESS to fans of this park, I visited it during a massive tree clean-up that left several of the sites looking like the aftermath of a tornado. However, the unique layout of the campground and the potential for some sites to be high on my list gave McCarthy Beach the boost it needed to be included.

This is a park for those who like to play in or on the water. The long sandy beach is a landmark in these parts, and the amenities clearly support all kinds of water-based activities. The campground is actually laid out on Side Lake, across the road from the big, long beach area. Both lakes have boat ramps, are excellent for fishing (Side Lake has two fishing piers for campers to use), and provide plenty of shoreline for exploration in canoes and kayaks.

There are 18 miles of hiking trails within the park, all stretched out along the interior of the northern half. These trails form long, interconnecting loops that traverse the glacial topography as they wind among towering stands of pine trees. Hikers can also hook up with the Taconite State Trail, which threads its way through this park and adjoining state forests. Birders can see more than 170 species of birds throughout the park at different times of the year.

Sturgeon Lake, nearly two miles across at its widest, offers anglers a chance to catch walleye, bass, northern pike, and panfish.

Now, onto the campgrounds. The first loop of sites, 1 through 13, are all electrical hookup sites; leave those for the RVs. The second loop gets a little better, but the configuration makes for tight sites with little privacy. The loop is intersected by three roads cutting it into quarters. These sites are all open with little understory, and they back onto other sites within this loop network. Site 42 is a large, open site with a clear

RATINGS

Beauty: ✿ ✿
Privacy: ✿ ✿ ✿
Spaciousness: ✿ ✿ ✿
Quiet: ✿ ✿
Security: ✿ ✿ ✿
Cleanliness: ✿ ✿ ✿

view of the lake—go for it in a pinch, and only if the last loop is full.

Ah, the last loop—very interesting! There's some major landscaping incorporated into some of the sites in this section. Many of them have extensive stone retaining walls that either define the tent and table area or secure the driveway or approaches to the sites. All the sites are spacious, so the landscaping further individualizes the campsite, making each one unique.

Site 47, on the roadway between the second and third loop, sits in front of an embankment fortified by a long, four-foot-tall wall of stones. The site sits above the roadway, offering a good view of the lake across the road. It's exposed so it's not very private. Sites 48 and 49 are inside the loop and about 50 yards from the lake. Since this loop angles back away from the lake slightly, these two sites are the closest to the water.

Site 50 is cut back into a grove of birch and aspen, a truly private yet spacious site outside the loop. Sites 51 and 52 are fairly close but roomy, with good understory screening. This area was undergoing extensive site work and tree removal but showed potential. Site 55 sits on a knoll with an elaborate stone retaining wall keeping it all together. The next three sites, 56 through 58, varied in size (site 56 is small but nice; 57 has a sloping camping area; and 58 is a long and narrow site). Site 59 features landscape timbers and a boulder-lined stairway—with a view of the lake filtered through a stand of pines.

This area was once covered in dense white and red pine forests. There are many small stands of these pines scattered throughout the campground and park. The carpet of needles on the forest floor was one of the thickest and softest coverings I have ever walked over. The pines in this area and those lining the county road that runs through the park reminded me of Lake Itasca at times.

At the extreme northwestern edge of the park lies Beatrice Lake Campground, a state forest area campground that could serve as a remote and even more rustic overflow option for the McCarthy Beach campground (it earns a listing of its own elsewhere in this section). Even if you don't intend to camp there,

KEY INFORMATION

ADDRESS: 7622 McCarthy Beach Road Side Lake, MN 55781

OPERATED BY: Minnesota DNR, Division of Parks and Recreation

INFORMATION: (218) 254-7979

OPEN: Year-round

SITES: 45 sites (17 with electricity, 14 rustic

ASSIGNMENT: First come, first served, unless reserved

REGISTRATION: Available at (866) 85-PARKS (72757), or online at www.stayatmnparks.com

FACILITIES: Showers, fishing pier, boat ramp, water, vault toilets

PARKING: Just past park office, and at start of first loop

FEES: $7 daily permit, $5 group, $25 annual; camping fee $15 semimodern, $18 electric hookup, $11 rustic, $8.50 nonrefundable reservation fee

ACTIVITIES: Swimming, fishing, boating, hiking, wildlife viewing

RESTRICTIONS: Pets: On 6-foot maximum leash Fires: In designated rings only Alcohol: Not allowed Vehicles: On designated trails or roads Other: Closed to nonregistered campers 10 p.m.–8 a.m.; use of weapons prohibited; no removal of flora or fauna from park

MAP

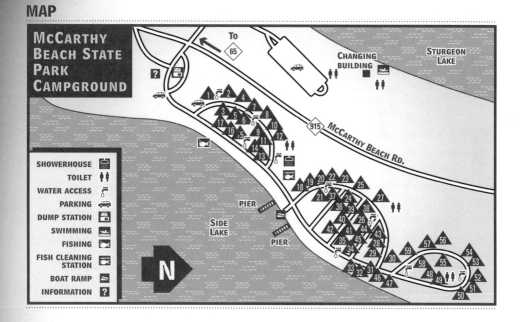

MᴄCᴀʀᴛʜʏ BEACH STATE PARK CAMPGROUND

To 65

CHANGING BUILDING

STURGEON LAKE

915 McCᴀʀᴛʜʏ BEACH RD.

PIER

SIDE LAKE

PIER

SHOWERHOUSE	🚿
TOILET	🚹🚺
WATER ACCESS	🚰
PARKING	🚗
DUMP STATION	🚽
SWIMMING	🏊
FISHING	🎣
FISH CLEANING STATION	🔪
BOAT RAMP	⛴
INFORMATION	❓

N

GETTING THERE

From Hibbing, take US 169 north to St. Louis CR 5. Take a left turn onto CR 5 (north) and go 15 miles to CR 65. Go left (west) about 1 mile to the park entrance on the right.

consider a drive up to Beatrice Lake. There is a small section of the road that is a red pine boulevard—the lanes are narrow and separated by a raised center section. Towering red pines grow right up to the roadway's edge, and the center corridor is thick with more majestic trees. It's quite a sight.

Make sure you bring your beach toys, fishing gear, and hiking boots on this camping trip!

MOSOMO POINT CAMPGROUND

THIS TENT-CAMPGROUND area is included for one simple reason: Mosomo Point caught my eye with its sheer simplicity and its incredibly large, long, and deep campsites! I felt as if I had pitched my tent in the sloping waterfront yard of a friend's cabin. There was enough room at the site I selected to pitch at least six tents and still have room for a round of lawn bowling. It was a pleasant surprise to me, because I had spent an entire summer in this area working as a student forester for Minnesota's DNR but had never visited the Lake Winnie area where Mosomo Point is located.

A wide open, grassy clearing, surrounded by towering red pines describes these campsites. Each site has ample grass-covered flat areas for numerous tents and myriad lawn games. The long, narrow, lakeside campsites are separated from the lake by a thick, reed-bound shoreline. The reed bed extends out into the lake for several yards. However, each site has direct access to the open water for fishing or launching a boat. Boaters have access to the waters of the Big Cut Foot Sioux Lake and First River that surrounds the point on three sides. From there the routes connecting to other lakes are almost endless.

The sites at Mosomo are the largest I've seen anywhere, bar none: state parks, state forest, and private campgrounds. There is no distinction between tent-only and RV sites, but because there are no RV facilities, the only advantage that Mosomo can offer is the incredibly long corridor beyond the driveway at each site. The standard-issue picnic table and grill-topped fire ring are the extent of "improvements" you'll find here. Each site's dense understory blocks the view from distant campsites and the road through the camp itself. These sites are off the chart for spaciousness and privacy!

> *This unimposing, serene, primitive campground sits in the heart of a beautiful, lake-filled forest.*

RATINGS

Beauty: ☆ ☆ ☆
Privacy: ☆ ☆ ☆ ☆ ☆
Spaciousness: ☆ ☆ ☆ ☆ ☆
Quiet: ☆ ☆ ☆
Security: ☆ ☆ ☆ ☆
Cleanliness: ☆ ☆ ☆ ☆

KEY INFORMATION

ADDRESS: Chippewa National Forest
Deer River District
P.O. Box 308
Deer River, MN 56636

OPERATED BY: Chippewa National Forest

INFORMATION: (218) 246-2123; www.fs.fed.us/r9/chippewa

OPEN: May 1–November 25

SITES: 22 primitive sites

ASSIGNMENT: First come, first served

REGISTRATION: Registration box at entrance to campground

FACILITIES: Vault toilets, water, recycling station, boat access

PARKING: At individual sites only

FEES: $14 single daily permit, $28 double

ACTIVITIES: Fishing and boating

RESTRICTIONS: **Pets:** All pets must be on a leash in campground
Fires: In designated fire rings only; collection of dead and down firewood only
Alcohol: Not allowed
Vehicles: ATV use is restricted to forest roads and trails not maintained for vehicle traffic
Other: Quiet time 10 p.m.–8 a.m.; no firearms or fireworks; specific restrictions may differ at individual campgrounds; 14-day stay limit

Of course the area is beautiful and picturesque—after all, it *is* the Chippewa National Forest. With more than 660,000 acres of forest, including the dominant white, red, and jack pine forests, dense stands of northern hardwoods, 700-plus lakes, 920-plus miles of streams, and 150,000 acres of wetlands, this forest is home to some of the best scenery, flora, and fauna that Minnesota has to offer.

Like most of the campgrounds in the Chippewa and Superior Forests, water plays a dominant role and is clearly the focal point of most of the recreational options. Whether for fishing or paddling, these modest campgrounds are the jumping-off places for enjoying hundreds of miles of streams, lakes, and far-away reaches of water. If the waters surrounding the Mosomo Point peninsula don't satisfy your aquatic needs, there's always Lake Winnibigoshish and its other watery neighbors. The not-so-mighty-at-this-point Mississippi River is still a relatively small stream where it spills out of Lake Winnie near here on its meandering flow southward. Mosomo Point is among several campgrounds in the immediate vicinity that are cut out of the forest—right at the water's edge. Many are connected by the same network of waterways, too.

Bird-watchers should be aware of the resident population of bald eagles that call the Chippewa home. Over 1,500 breeding pairs have been counted in these trees. It's not uncommon to hear the imposing *whoof-whoof-whoof* of gigantic wing beats overhead as these mighty birds power out from the shadows and swoop out over the meadows.

The Cut Foot Sioux area also has numerous non-motorized trails and plenty of local wildlife (osprey, loon, deer) to keep animal- and bird-watchers busy.

The lowest mark on this campground's report card is the nominal quietness of the site. The point itself is as quiet as it can be. However, motor boat traffic from nearby lodges and the fluctuating level of traffic noise from the state highway has the potential to create a subtle and almost unnoticeable commercial drone in the background. That annoyance lasts only until that first loon begins to call. It seemed to me that its call echoed within my tall pine hideaway all night long.

MAP

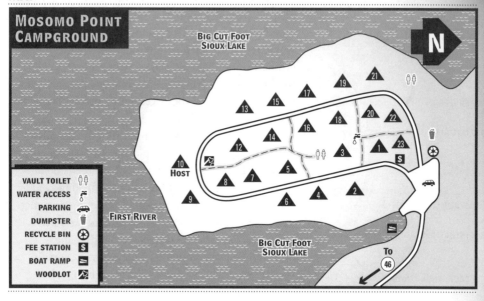

MOSOMO POINT CAMPGROUND

Big Cut Foot Sioux Lake

N

13 15 17 19 21
16 18 20 22
14 12 8 7 5 3 1 23
10 HOST 9 6 4 2

LEGEND

VAULT TOILET	👭
WATER ACCESS	🚰
PARKING	🚙
DUMPSTER	🗑
RECYCLE BIN	♻
FEE STATION	$
BOAT RAMP	⛵
WOODLOT	🪵

FIRST RIVER

Big Cut Foot Sioux Lake

To 46

GETTING THERE

From the town of Bena, take US 2 east 1.5 miles to CR 9. Turn left (north) and go 11 miles to MN 46. Turn left (north) on MN 46; and drive 6.6 miles to the campground sign. Turn left into the campground.

NORTH STAR CAMPGROUND

> *This spacious campground is right on one of the most scenic drives in Minnesota.*

I HADN'T BEEN SEEKING this campground when I sped by it heading back south after a long weekend of checking out the northeastern section of the Chippewa Forest. Instead, I was enjoying the 200-year-old pine forests and other natural sites along the Northwoods Scenic Byway, a beautiful, pine-tree corridor along MN 38 that extends 40 miles between Grand Rapids and Big Fork. Don't expect a lot of commercial amenities along this route—take the opportunity to explore side roads throughout the Chippewa National Forest and the George Washington State Forest.

I saw the National Forest Campground sign and immediately fanned through my pile of reference papers and maps on the seat beside me. North Star Campground hadn't jumped off the page at me the first time around because its list of amenities pretty much stopped at "lake." What a lucky break for us all. North Star Campground is definitely a good find.

The 36 sites at North Star Campground are laid out along a bisected kidney-shaped loop nestled into an aspen and balsam fir forest sandwiched between the state road and the shores of the lake.

Sites 1 and 2 are long, narrow keyhole sites that open up to a stand of aspens and balsam fir at the end of long driveways. Site 3 is wheelchair-accessible off the inside of the loop but centrally located to facilities and the lake itself. There is no site 4—look for the firewood bin where you'd expect another tent site.

Site 5 is another long, narrow site and neighbors the campground host at site 6. Sites 8 and 9 overlook North Star Lake. Both sites are open to the road, but the view compensates for the lack of privacy. There is also a trail down to the lake just before the driveway to 7.

Just before site 9 there is a turn-off to the parking area at the trailhead that leads to the swimming area at the beach. The campsite right after the parking lot is

RATINGS

Beauty: ✿ ✿ ✿
Privacy: ✿ ✿ ✿
Spaciousness: ✿ ✿ ✿ ✿
Quiet: ✿ ✿ ✿
Security: ✿ ✿ ✿ ✿
Cleanliness: ✿ ✿ ✿ ✿

on a slight rise surrounded by more understory than grass as in most other sites at North Star Lake.

Site 10, although it is located inside the loop, is far enough off the road to reward campers with more privacy than most other sites in this loop. Sites 12 through 14 are fairly open but are especially friendly and spacious sites nonetheless. The angled and staggered driveways give each site ample screening from others and from the roadway. Sites 15 and 16 are keyhole-designed driveways and sites—a plus because the entrances to these two sites sit opposite one another. The rest of the sites in this left (southern) half of the loop all retain the sense of private and spaciousness that is most characteristic of the campground. Site 19 is especially appealing if only for the fact that it's back in the woods and is the last site on the outside edge. Although I didn't detect any noise, I would suspect that these last few sites might put campers within heightened earshot of road noise from MN 38, just outside the campgrounds.

The other half of the loop, the northern section, is cut through a younger stand of aspen and spruce and fir trees. Most of these sites are in the keyhole style, similar to those in the other half of the loop. The inside loop offers a pleasant change—its sites are cut out of a dense understory and are quite private and very well protected from each other and the road. Much of the screening between campsites and the background understory is provided by a young spruce forest that blankets this area.

Sites 22 through 31 are similar in layout and appearance. Site 28 is the wheelchair-accessible site and is centrally located within the loop, connected by foot trails and easily within reach of the toilets and water pump.

Site 32 is the first spot in this half of the loop that could be described as being on the lake. It's a beautiful campsite overlooking North Star Lake that is accessible via a stairway and trail down to the shoreline. In fact, all the sites along the ridge above the lake have stairways or trails leading right down to the water. Of these sites, 33 is the most exposed. A trail cuts to the lake between sites 35 and 36.

KEY INFORMATION

ADDRESS: Marcell District, Chippewa National Forest 49554 MN 38 Marcell, MN 56657

OPERATED BY: Chippewa National Forest

INFORMATION: (218) 832-3161 or www.fs.fd.us/r9/ chippewa

OPEN: Year-round

SITES: 36 rustic sites (RV or tent)

ASSIGNMENT: First come, first served; reservations for 28 sites by calling (877) 444-6777 or online at www.reserveusa.com

REGISTRATION: Registration box at entrance

FACILITIES: Vault toilet, drinking water, playground, boat ramp

PARKING: By swimming area

FEES: $12 single daily permit, $24 double; $9 reservation fee

ACTIVITIES: Swimming, fishing, canoeing

RESTRICTIONS: Pets: All pets must be on a leash in campground
Fires: In designated rings only; collection of dead and down firewood only
Alcohol: Not allowed
Vehicles: ATV use on forest roads and trails not maintained for vehicle traffic
Other: Quiet time 10 p.m.–8 a.m.; no firearms or fireworks; 14-day stay limit

MAP

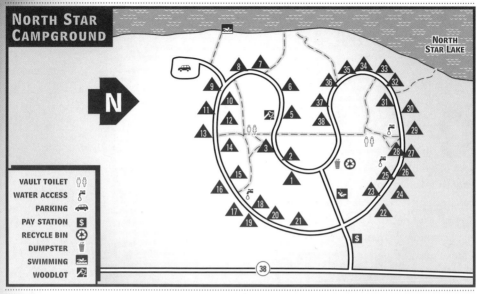

NORTH STAR CAMPGROUND

NORTH STAR LAKE

VAULT TOILET	♂♀
WATER ACCESS	⌐
PARKING	🚗
PAY STATION	$
RECYCLE BIN	♻
DUMPSTER	🗑
SWIMMING	🏊
WOODLOT	🌲

GETTING THERE

From Marcell, head south on MN 38 3 miles to the campground on the right (western) side of road.

The road turns away from the lake at site 36. The remaining sites are uniformly narrow compared to the majority of the keyhole sites in the campground.

North Star Lake is over 1,000 acres in size and is at least 3 miles long. It appears on the map as an irregularly edged, inverted Y. It is known for its myriad sheltered bays and ever-wavering shoreline. There are numerous sandy and grassy beaches throughout. Anglers can try their luck catching walleye, northern, and muskie pike as well as bluegills, crappie, and bass.

North Star Lake is like a small, simply faceted gem sitting unnoticed in a big jewelry box.

OWEN LAKE STATE FOREST CAMPGROUND

OWEN **LAKE IS ONE** of those rare finds that makes doing a camping guide so rewarding. Initially I had traveled to this somewhat bleak area of Minnesota, a region of vast spruce swamps and endless miles of nondescript forest roads to check out Scenic State Park. I was underwhelmed by that campground, so I decided to see if the state forest sites were as pleasant in this remote area as they were elsewhere. I am so glad I did.

Owen Lake is a beautiful, irregularly shaped northern lake with several bays and bumps along its shoreline. Nestled under a healthy stand of red pines on a peninsula jutting out from the lake's western shore is the state forest campground.

Getting to Owen Lake means several miles of paved, then gravel, roads through impressive stands of red pine. The campground is likewise under an umbrella of red pine with an understory of both young red and jack pine. All the sites are laid out along a long, narrow loop that extends toward the peninsula's point. Sites are spread apart nicely to allow for privacy, and even those away from the lake are an easy foot walk across the loop to the beach.

Site 1 is in a grove of red pine but not situated close enough to the lake to claim that as a feature. Sites 2 and 3 back up to the lake and could be a combination or group site because there is little screening between the two. Sites 4 and 5 are long, narrow sites that go back into the pines for spacious and private camping. Site 6 is on the lake but exposed to the road.

The nicest site on the lake is 7, but don't expect to camp there—it's used all summer by the campground host. You'll have to settle for site 8, off by itself amid the jack pine understory.

Just past site 8, the loop swings to the left, with a parking turnout on the right. This is the trailhead for

> *This modest campground on a red pine–forested peninsula is the epitome of the perfect lakeside campsite.*

RATINGS

Beauty: ✪ ✪ ✪ ✪
Privacy: ✪ ✪ ✪ ✪ ✪
Spaciousness: ✪ ✪ ✪ ✪ ✪
Quiet: ✪ ✪ ✪
Security: ✪ ✪ ✪
Cleanliness: ✪ ✪ ✪ ✪

KEY INFORMATION

ADDRESS: c/o Scenic State Park
56956 Scenic
Highway 7
Bigfork, MN 56628

OPERATED BY: Managed by Scenic
State Park; see also:
Minnesota DNR,
Division of Forestry
(651) 296-6157

INFORMATION: (218) 743-3362

OPEN: Year-round

SITES: 20 rustic campsites

ASSIGNMENT: First come, first
served

REGISTRATION: No reservations

FACILITIES: Vault toilet, water,
picnic pavilion

PARKING: Across from picnic
area; at trailhead to
site 9; just before site
11

FEES: $10 per night

ACTIVITIES: Fishing, swimming,
canoeing, kayaking

RESTRICTIONS: Pets: Must be kept
on leash
Fires: Must be in
cleared areas at least
5 feet around and
built less than 3 feet
in diameter
Alcohol: Not allowed
Vehicles: No motor-
ized vehicles on any
nonmotorized trails
or in posted areas
that prohibit use
Other: Hunting and
firearms only in
posted areas; camp-
ing possible in
undeveloped areas
(special rules apply);
check information
station for seasonal
and special
restrictions

sites 9 and 10. These sites require that you carry all your gear into camp. It will be worth it—even if it means lugging the 50-pound cooler 50 yards! This peninsula has an open understory with a mature red pine forest and a panoramic view of the lake.

Site 9 is just off the road and therefore more immediately accessible. It is far enough from site 10 to offer more privacy than most, but expect some trail use as campers at site 10 and other visitors explore this point.

Site 10, what can I say? It's under a tall stand of straight, lean red pines with an open, pine needle–covered forest floor. There are a few jack pines scattered throughout, and scattered paper birch add north country charm. The end of the peninsula rises to form a modest knoll above the water. The campground is completely exposed to those approaching from the main loop, but it's so spacious that one can turn toward the lake and forget about everytthing else. Water and toilets are back on the loop, only a campsite down from the trailhead.

The lake to the east is very inviting for canoeing or kayaking. It appears to offer several miles of unde-veloped shoreline typical of most northern lakes. Immediately across from the campground there are a few cabins lining the shore.

Site 11 begins the series of campsites on the loop away from the water. There is a private residence with a small pulp-timber operation behind site 11. This spot, however, does sit in the red pines and is screened from the private property beyond.

Sites 13 and 14 are basic campgrounds and feature those common amenities of picnic table, fire ring, and tent space. Sites 15 through 18 are big, open sites and therefore roomy but very private compared to others. Sites 19 and 20 are close to the road and nondescript.

It is truly unfortunate that there are not more sites like number 10. Plan your trip to arrive early and secure it for a real camping treat.

There are scores of fishing and boating lakes, many with campgrounds, surrounding Owen Lake. The George Washington State Forest, in which Owen Lake is located, is just northeast of the Chippewa National

MAP

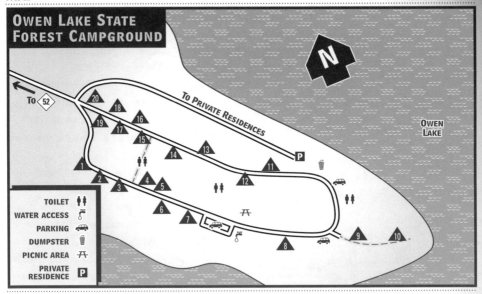

OWEN LAKE STATE FOREST CAMPGROUND

To 52

To Private Residences

OWEN LAKE

TOILET	
WATER ACCESS	
PARKING	
DUMPSTER	
PICNIC AREA	
PRIVATE RESIDENCE	P

Forest's extensive lake region. All these areas offer camping, but none offer the beauty and grandness of site 10 at Owen Lake. Treat yourself: check it out.

GETTING THERE

From Bigfork, take Scenic Highway/CR 7 southeast 10 miles to CR 340. Turn left (east) and go about 7 miles to CR 52; turn left (north) and follow the signs for about 2 miles to the campground entrance on the right.

SAVANNAH PORTAGE STATE PARK CAMPGROUND

> *Relive the lifestyle of voyagers of yore while you enjoy northwoods camping in lake country.*

YOU CAN LOOK at Savannah Portage from a couple of perspectives: you can observe the northwoods lake country sculpted by glaciers that formed lakes, bogs, and rolling hillside; or you can envision brightly clad French fur traders and other voyageurs portaging heavy canoes and gear half a dozen miles through shallow streams and across expansive mud flats—and then through several miles of virgin northern forest. Such is the dual personality of this park.

Glacially speaking, Savannah Portage is an example of how some river country was formed. When huge ice fields retreated, they left great moraine fields at their leading edge. These ridges of rock blocked flowages from melting ice until at some weak point they broke through, creating channels through which rivers could run. These connecting river systems, first learned and traveled by the Native Americans, became the water routes and portages that ultimately linked the Great Lakes and points east to the Mississippi River and the great interior of North America.

There are many places within this park to actually experience what these early canoeists went through to move their boats and gear across the continent. There are several lakes within the park's boundaries as well as remote camping sites that are only accessible by a walking trail to the lake and then a paddle to the site. To really feel like a voyageur of yore, one could carry the canoe and camping gear from a trailhead parking lot to the remote lake and imagine what a six-mile portage would feel like.

The 64 campsites are laid out between two elongated loops on the southwestern edge of Lake Shumway. A winding road through a random spattering of glacial hills covered in older aspen and surrounded by tamarack swamps greets visitors as they approach these sites.

RATINGS

Beauty: ✿ ✿ ✿
Privacy: ✿ ✿ ✿
Spaciousness: ✿ ✿ ✿
Quiet: ✿ ✿ ✿
Security: ✿ ✿ ✿
Cleanliness: ✿ ✿ ✿

The campground is situated on a high ridge under an umbrella of aspens mixed with balsam fir trees. The sites are typical state-park issue: picnic table, fire ring, and place for tent. Some sites are open in a stand of pines (site 3); some have long, narrow driveways (site 7). Most of the sites in the first loop are electrical, so expect them to be in high demand by the mechanized campers. Once you get half way around the loop, you begin to see the lake through the trees. Sites 26 and 27 are situated on the outside edge of the loop, with the lake behind them. A trail extends from the road just before site 27 and leads to an intersection with a trail that continues around Lake Shumway and also connects to other trail systems in the park. These two sites are especially choice spots and will go quickly. The rest of the sites to the end of the first loop are also electrical sites.

The second loop is laid out parallel to the lake, not right at its edge but viewable through the trees. The first sites in this loop are exposed, right off the roadway, providing no privacy. Lakeside sites 41 through 45 are small but quaint, each overlooking the lake beyond the screen of trees. The exception is site 42; it's across the road and has a pull-through driveway because it is one of two wheelchair-accessible sites in this park.

There is a rental cabin right off the loop by site 52. The rest of the sites along the upper edge of the loop are typical, with the exception of site 58, which is off by itself and private. Likewise, site 60 is situated up from the road and right across from site 61, which is also accessible to disabled campers.

The group site is a spacious, grassy opening across from the road running through the first loop. Sites 62 through 64 are exposed to each other beneath a canopy of mature red and white pines. Site 63 backs up to site 60 in the second loop, and 64 is off of to the west with woods as its backdrop.

Even though this park's theme is based on the voyageur heritage, it could easily be called a hiker's park as well. There are more than 22 miles of hiking trails, many of which encircle the lakes within the park. You can even hike part of the original Savannah Portage—modernized with a wood plank walkway through one of the swampy areas.

KEY INFORMATION

ADDRESS: 55626 Lake Place McGregor, MN 55760

OPERATED BY: Minnesota DNR, Division of Parks and Recreation

INFORMATION: (218) 426-3271

OPEN: Year-round

SITES: 63 semimodern (16 with electricity), 7 backpack, 1 canoe; primitive group camp

ASSIGNMENT: First come, first served, unless reserved

REGISTRATION: Available at (866) 85-PARKS (72757), or online at www.stay-atmnparks.com

FACILITIES: Boat ramp, dock, fishing pier, play field, restroom, showers, water

PARKING: Throughout grounds

FEES: $7 daily permit, $5 group, $25 annual; camping fee $15 semimodern, $18 electric hookup, $11 rustic, $8.50 nonrefundable reservation fee

ACTIVITIES: Swimming, fishing, canoeing, kayaking, hiking, wildlife photography

RESTRICTIONS: Pets: On 6-foot maximum leash Fires: In designated rings only Alcohol: Not allowed Vehicles: On designated trails or roads Other: Closed to nonregistered campers 10 p.m.– 8 a.m.

MAP

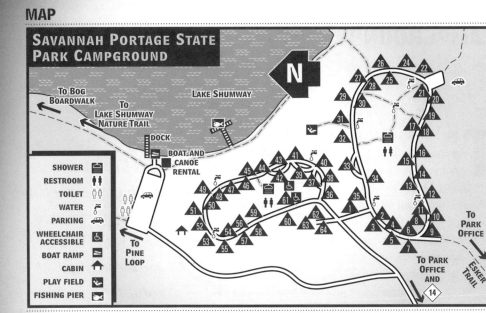

SAVANNAH PORTAGE STATE PARK CAMPGROUND

To Bog Boardwalk
To Lake Shumway Nature Trail
Lake Shumway
DOCK
BOAT AND CANOE RENTAL

SHOWER	
RESTROOM	
TOILET	
WATER	
PARKING	
WHEELCHAIR ACCESSIBLE	
BOAT RAMP	
CABIN	
PLAY FIELD	
FISHING PIER	

To Pine Loop
To Park Office
To Park Office And
Esker Trail
14

GETTING THERE

From McGregor, take US 65 north to Aitkin CR 14. Turn right and continue north on CR 14, 10 miles to the park entrance. It's another 0.5 miles to the campground.

The park lies within the boundary of Savannah State Forest, so trails extend out beyond the park, creating a network that offers hikers many multilooped routes, some leading to remote lakes.

The lakes have resident northern pike, trout, bass, and panfish. I first camped at Savannah Portage more than 20 years ago and spent a whole day just whiling away the time in my canoe. Such water activities and a good set of hiking boots will keep campers at Savannah Portage primed with options throughout their stay.

SAWBILL LAKE CAMPGROUND

THE **SAWBILL TRAIL**—it's got that boundary-waters ring to it, like the Gunflint and the Echo, names that conjure up canoeing across long, pine-forested lakes in God's country. There are many campsites stretched out along the perimeter of the Boundary Waters Canoe Area Wilderness (WCAW) but few nicer and more convenient than the Sawbill Lake Campground, sitting almost halfway along the BWCAW's southern boundary.

While most campers are probably overnighting at Sawbill before heading out on that canoe trip of a lifetime, there are probably as many others who have come to enjoy the waterways of Sawbill Lake and beyond for a weekend of paddling. The campground features plenty of amenities to satisfy even the noncanoeist in a group: bass and northern pike fishing off the barrier-free fishing pier; a short nature trail along the lake and looped through the campgrounds; and even a genuine northwoods canoe outfitter right next door—a real hub of activity offering canoes, paddles, showers, groceries—and throngs of canoers from all across the country.

The Sawbill Lake campsite is a long loop divided into quarters along a ridge above the lake. The first campsite sits right off the entrance and seems more like a sentry post than a campsite—in location, not features. It's right across from the canoe storage area, a convenient, shoreside area where you can keep your canoe instead of lugging it up to camp every day.

The terrain is hilly and covered in a mix of spruce and pines. The campground road climbs up a ridge as it leaves site 1 and presents sites 2 and 3 off a Y driveway on the right. These sites are in a stand of birch and balsam but are otherwise open, offering little privacy. Site 4 is likewise open and sits across from site 5, which does overlook the lake. This is a site worth noting for the big red pine trees throughout.

> *This hub of activity is a major entry point for canoe trips into the BWCAW and has northwoods charm—a beautiful lake, towering pines, and memorable scenery.*

RATINGS

Beauty: ✩ ✩ ✩
Privacy: ✩ ✩ ✩
Spaciousness: ✩ ✩ ✩
Quiet: ✩ ✩ ✩
Security: ✩ ✩ ✩
Cleanliness: ✩ ✩ ✩

KEY INFORMATION

ADDRESS: c/o Tofte Ranger District
P.O. Box 2157
Tofte, MN 55615

OPERATED BY: Superior National Forest

INFORMATION: (218) 663-7280 or www.fs.fed.us/r9/superior

OPEN: Year-round

SITES: 50 campsites

ASSIGNMENT: First come, first served

REGISTRATION: Fee station at entrance to campground

FACILITIES: Vault toilet, water, trash container, canoe storage area

PARKING: At fishing pier and to right of campground entrance at Sawbill Outfitters

FEES: $12 daily permit (maximum of 8 people and 2 cars per site, third vehicle is $6 per day)

ACTIVITIES: Fishing, swimming, canoeing, hiking

RESTRICTIONS: **Pets:** Must be on leash and under control, both in camp and on trails
Fires: In fire rings unless otherwise allowed, such as in backcountry sites
Alcohol: Not allowed
Vehicles: ATV use restricted to roads and trails not maintained for vehicle traffic
Other: 14-day stay limit

Sites 6 through 9 are all decent sites in size and location, each being a short distance from the road and each under a canopy of giant red pines. These are older forests without much understory. Tent sites 14 and 16 through 18 border the lake and are set back from the road but still quite open, meaning minimal privacy. However, the view down to the lake through the rustic red columns of red pine trees gives these sites their real value. Site 13 is very typical of the sites throughout the park, although it is on the small side.

Sites 19 through 21 are close to the road, but the stands of red pine are impressive. The fact that there is minimal understory or other screening between the sites is unimportant because the canopy above is so impressive that no one's bothering to look into other camps—they are gazing into the treetops.

A trail crossing the road just before 21 is part of the campground loop that follows the lake from the canoe storage area to the shoreline below site 21. It cuts through to the outside loop at site 34 and follows the campground road back down past site 45 before it cuts back through the campground to the lake just below campsites 10 and 12.

Sites 22 and 23 are on opposite sides of the road—open, but secluded. Site 24 is a small site but is off by itself inside the curve as the road cuts away from the lake and the remaining 26 sites.

At the tip of the curve sits site 26, with its long, narrow driveway leading to a very isolated campsite. Better to stay at this one than its neighbor: site 27 is way too exposed and sits at the Y intersection with the outer campground road and the spur to CR 2 that heads north from the campsites.

Campsites 30 through 39 are staggered along the loop with most of the sites on the outside of the circle. These sites, with a few exceptions, are long and narrow with a pleasing understory dominated by balsam fir. Sites to avoid are 35 (very small) and 36 (open and in a clearing).

By site 44, the forest is mainly white pine. The site to shy away from here is 49 because it backs up, nearly tent-stake-to-tent-stake, with site 6 on the first loop. The sites have an open understory and a direct line

MAP

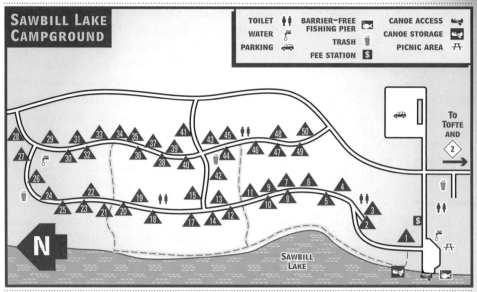

SAWBILL LAKE CAMPGROUND

TOILET	BARRIER-FREE FISHING PIER	CANOE ACCESS
WATER	TRASH	CANOE STORAGE
PARKING	FEE STATION	PICNIC AREA

SAWBILL LAKE

N

To TOFTE AND
2

from driveway to driveway right through the middle of the camping area. The last site in this campground is 50, a big site alone among the pines.

As either a canoe country starting-off point or as a base camp for local exploring, Sawbill Lake is a great northwoods canoe country campground.

GETTING THERE

From Duluth, go north along the lake to Tofte. In Tofte, take a left (north) on CR 2 (Sawbill Trail). Go about 25 miles CR 2 to the campground entrance. Turn left toward the boat-launch area and then right into the campground.

SPLIT ROCK LIGHTHOUSE STATE PARK CAMPGROUND

"These beautiful, remote campsites are nestled along the north shore of Lake Superior with easy access to the historic Split Rock Lighthouse."

SPLIT ROCK LIGHTHOUSE may be a stretch for "drive-to" tent camping because most of the sites are at least 400 feet from the parking lot. But because there are four sites within a few hundred yards of parking, and because this is prime north shore camping, I decided to list it.

The shoreline here is typical of the entire Minnesota section of Lake Superior. Sheer cliffs drop abruptly to the cold, clear waters of the great lake sometimes called Gitchi Gumee. Birch and spruce trees line the shore and extend all the way to the tops of "mountains" more than 1,000 feet tall. It's an area that was formed from ancient lava flows, covered in the sediment of great prehistoric seas, and then sculpted by glacial forces into its present form.

The ruggedness of this shoreline challenged the timber companies harvesting the mature stands of pine that lined these shores. After several ships were lost around the Split Rock area in the early 1900s, a lighthouse and fog signal was contracted in 1909. That structure was in operation until 1969. In 1976 the Minnesota Historical Society began operating the site as a tourist attraction and continues to do so today.

The lighthouse attracts visitors to this area, but it's the camping that will keep them there for at least a night or two. The sites are off a trail that runs along the lake, above and parallel to the shoreline. Four sites are right off the parking lot overlooking the lake, a half-dozen more are off the trail that extends up a draw, and the rest are located on either side of a trail that continues north. The farthest campsite is about 2,000 feet from the parking lot.

These are rustic sites, and each is assigned a large, easy-to-maneuver utility cart. When not hauling gear, it's a good rain cover for firewood.

RATINGS

Beauty: ✿ ✿ ✿ ✿
Privacy: ✿ ✿ ✿ ✿ ✿
Spaciousness: ✿ ✿ ✿ ✿
Quiet: ✿ ✿ ✿
Security: ✿ ✿ ✿ ✿ ✿
Cleanliness: ✿ ✿ ✿

Site 1 is off one of the main hiking trails that are part of the network through the park and beyond. It parallels the parking lot, and this site is only a few steps away. It is tucked back off the trail and up a small rise, mostly unseen from the trail and any other sites. Sites 2 and 3 are spread out along the Little Two Harbors Trail, perched like natural balconies high above the tree-covered shoreline below. Each site is exposed to that foot traffic but separated by distance and some vegetation from each other. It's a modest transition from car camping to walk-in camping, a good opportunity to test your wings out on this kind of venture. Site 4 sits on a rock-bordered knoll above the trail and the shower house with a view of the parking lot and the trail intersection that leads to the rest of the campsites. Up beyond the rock ledge that forms a backdrop for this site is a lofty perch that overlooks the lake—a great vista of the entire far western end of Lake Superior.

If you are going to enjoy the more distant sites, you'll need to make trips with one of the large-wheeled, high-volume utility carts with big crossbar handles. They should easily traverse the changing topography of these sites along the lake and up the slope.

Sites 5 through 10 are off the eight-foot paved pathway that weaves up from the main trail toward the top of the ridge. The sites are spacious and fairly open but well screened from the other sites. The farther you climb, the closer you are to the north shore highway—and its traffic noise. The sites along the lake have that sound muffled by the trees and drowned out by the wave action along the shore below.

That same paved trail drops and weaves downward toward sites 11 through 20. Site 11 is just off the trail to the left, just past the intersection to sites 5 through 10. This site shares the same rocky perch mentioned in 5 because it, too, is set back from the edge of a rocky ridge directly above the lake.

About 150 feet farther down the lake trail you'll find campsites 11 through 20. These are staggered off the main pathway, half toward the water, half on the slope side. Sites 12, 14, and 15 are all at the base of a 900-foot mound (a trail goes around its base) and are nestled into the dense birch forest that covers this

KEY INFORMATION

ADDRESS:	3755 Split Rock Lighthouse Road Two Harbors, MN 55616
OPERATED BY:	Minnesota DNR, Division of Parks and Recreation
INFORMATION:	(218) 226-6377
OPEN:	Year-round
SITES:	20 rustic, walk-in sites only
ASSIGNMENT:	First come, first served, unless reserved
REGISTRATION:	Available at (866) 85-PARKS (72757), or reserve online at www.stayatmn parks.com
FACILITIES:	Showers, drinking water, toilet (facility open early May–early October)
PARKING:	Just before trailhead to campsites
FEES:	$7 daily permit, $5 group permit, $25 annual permit; camping fee $11 rustic; $8.50 nonrefundable reservation fee
ACTIVITIES:	Hiking, beach-combing, lighthouse
RESTRICTIONS:	**Pets:** On 6-foot maximum leash **Fires:** In designated rings only **Alcohol:** Not allowed **Vehicles:** On designated trails or roads **Other:** Closed to nonregistered campers 10 p.m.–8 a.m.; use of weapons prohibited; no removal of flora or fauna from park

MAP

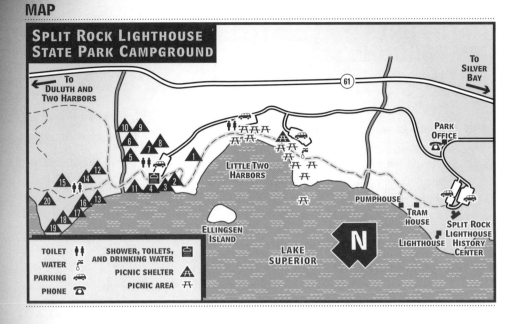

SPLIT ROCK LIGHTHOUSE STATE PARK CAMPGROUND

To DULUTH AND TWO HARBORS

To SILVER BAY

61

PARK OFFICE

LITTLE TWO HARBORS

PUMPHOUSE

TRAM HOUSE

SPLIT ROCK LIGHTHOUSE

LIGHTHOUSE HISTORY CENTER

ELLINGSEN ISLAND

LAKE SUPERIOR

N

	TOILET			SHOWER, TOILETS, AND DRINKING WATER	
	WATER			PICNIC SHELTER	
	PARKING			PICNIC AREA	
	PHONE				

GETTING THERE

From Two Harbors, take MN 61 about 18 miles north to the park entrance on the right.

entire area. Site 13 is a short jaunt off toward the water, while sites 16 and 17 split off a common trail spur another 150 feet beyond the last site. Sites 18 and 19 are on spurs that head out to a point overlooking the lake, and 20 is at the end of the trail. Site 20 sits close to the steep, descending slopes of the mound rising just west of it. The distance to this site from the parking lot is a little more than a third of a mile.

This campsite will give newcomers to camping a chance to experience more remote, self-sufficient camping. The extra effort is well worth it.

Split Rock Lighthouse State Park offers sightings of deer, moose, black bear (be sure to read the "Camping in Bear Country" information provided at the park), beaver, and more. There are many vistas overlooking the lake, so you should explore hiking options while camping here. You can use the trail system to hike from the campground to the lighthouse site or to connect with the Day Hill Trail that encircles the hill up by the tent sites. There is a spur leading to an overlook on top.

This campsite has an approach and access that take a little stamina; the reward for this challenge is north shore scenic Minnesota camping.

SULLIVAN LAKE STATE FOREST CAMPGROUND

SULLIVAN LAKE IS typical of most of the state forest campgrounds in northern Minnesota: mostly undeveloped, having only basic facilities, and usually remote, situated on a lake or river. The main focus is usually fishing or water recreation. And for that, Sullivan Lake is no different. These and other state forests campgrounds are just that—campgrounds. They are surrounded by the forest and presume that campers will entertain themselves. Like a typical site, they offer a tent space, picnic table, and fire ring. Really, what more do you need?

Sullivan Lake is a long, narrow, north–south aligned northwoods body of water. The edges are lined with rushes, and the shoreline is forested mostly in birch, aspen, and evergreens (spruce and firs). There are a few towering white and red pines poking their crowns above the canopy. It's one of those lakes that is nondescript yet offers all the aromas and sounds of the great north woods. A stream entering the northern tip from a boggy area feeds the lake. A small, footprint-shaped island lies just offshore from the first few campsites and invites a stop for break and a picnic or exploration. All these nuances combine to form a very pleasant setting, a setting that satisfies. It's great for a few nights of tent camping.

Sites 1 and 2 are on a knoll above the lake. Site 1 is closest to the road and entrance and doesn't have as nice a view of the lake as site 2. These two sites are open and grassy with a few clusters of trees separating them from each other. However, the openness and proximity of the sites to each other gives this the look and feel of a group site—if not officially, at least practically—and therefore it's suited for a larger group of campers with several tents. If you want privacy, go to the sites farther along this spur.

> *This is a basic yet serene setting on a northern lake halfway between the North Shore and the Boundary Waters Canoe Area Wildnerness.*

RATINGS

Beauty: ☆ ☆ ☆
Privacy: ☆ ☆
Spaciousness: ☆ ☆ ☆ ☆
Quiet: ☆ ☆ ☆ ☆
Security: ☆ ☆ ☆
Cleanliness: ☆ ☆ ☆ ☆

ADDRESS: c/o Split Rock Lighthouse State Park
3755 Split Rock
Lighthouse Road
Two Harbors, MN
55616

OPERATED BY: Managed by Split Rock Lighthouse State Park; see also: Minnesota DNR, Division of Forestry (651) 296-6157

INFORMATION: (218) 226-6377

OPEN: Year-round

SITES: 11 rustic sites

ASSIGNMENT: First come, first served

REGISTRATION: Reservations not available

FACILITIES: Vault toilet, water pump, boat ramp

PARKING: At boat ramp and just before entrance to campground spur

FEES: $10 per night

ACTIVITIES: Lake fishing, boating, hiking trail

RESTRICTIONS: Pets: Must be kept on leash
Fires: Must be in cleared areas at least 5 feet around and built less than 3 feet in diameter
Alcohol: Not allowed
Vehicles: No motorized vehicles on non-motorized trails or in areas that prohibit use
Other: Hunting and firearms only in posted areas; camping possible in undeveloped areas

The understory throughout the campgrounds is generally a dense cover of alders, fir, and birch with boulders strewn throughout. Site 3 is a beautiful camping area that features a site that drops down from the parking area and affords campers access to the lake via a short trail spur. Following the lakeshore south will connect hikers to the trail that circumnavigates the lake.

Site 4 is quite small—a narrow, open site—but one that overlooks the lake and is actually quite a pleasant little tent site. The tent sites are far apart, another characteristic of state forest sites.

Sites 5 and 6 have that inviting RV look in that they are very close to the road and have a wayside rest appearance and appeal to them. They are right across from site 9, the wheelchair-accessibile site. Site 7 is close to the road but perched above the lake.

The campground road ends in a cul-de-sac with a campsite off its tip. Site 8 is therefore the most private site in the campground—except that it sits at the head of the hiking trail that extends around the lake. Parking your vehicle in front of the site creates a visual barrier from hikers and drivers.

All these sites have access to Sullivan Lake and therefore encourage canoeing and kayaking. I don't remember any notable development occurring on the lake, so once you are on the water you have a tree-lined lake all to yourself (and the other campers).

Although you are about 20 miles inland from the North Shore and all its natural amenities, there are several county roads to explore, ultimately leading to points along Lake Superior. In fact, you are fairly close to other forest campsites, but this one made more of an impression on me. Also, it would be a good campground to stay at while exploring the waterfalls and trails in the closer state parks (Gooseberry Falls, Split Rock Lighthouse, Tettegouche).

Not only that, but you are also only about 20 miles south of MN 1, which leads to Ely and the Boundary Waters Canoe Area Wildnerness (BWCAW) country. The nice thing about Sullivan is that you have nearly that same feel but no need for permits and don't feel like you're at a checkpoint.

MAP

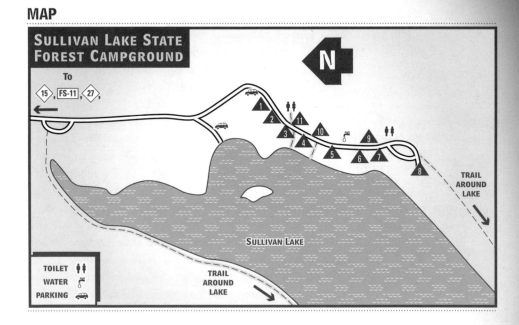

GETTING THERE

From Two Harbors, take
CR 2 north 27 miles to
FS 11 (County Road 15).
Turn left (west) and go 0.5
miles, then turn left again
(south) and go 0.5 miles to
the campground.

TETTEGOUCHE STATE PARK CAMPGROUND

> *Take your pick from a Lake Superior shoreline, numerous rapids, cascades, and the state's tallest waterfall, to rugged, mountain-like terrain, and northern hardwood forests.*

RIGHT OFF THE TOP I have to say that Tettegouche State Park is one of my favorites! It's got one of the very best tent sites I've seen anywhere in this state. The rivers, waterfalls (including Minnesota's tallest), and rapids are indescribable, and the hiking is some of the best in the region—what's not to like about tent camping here? Very little!

I remember this area from many years ago, before it was called Tettegouche. I had come here from Minneapolis to hike and enjoy the incredible waterfalls and cascading rivers. I don't remember camping here being an option way back then, so the opportunity to review this park was a real treat for me. One of the reasons for adding it to the state's inventory of parks is its diversity.

Like most property converted to parks, this one has its roots in Minnesota's timber industry. Once the timber was harvested, the lumber company sold the area to a group of Duluth businessmen—the Tettegouche Club—to be used as a fishing retreat. It changed hands a number of times until it became a park in 1979.

Outflows of lava (along a rift line that stretches all the way to Kansas), layers of seabed sediment, and scouring by several glacial periods all helped create the park we enjoy today. The drainage patterns of this part of the North Shore created the numerous waterfalls and cascades for which this and other parks in the area are known.

Whitetail deer, snowshoe hares, and 140 species of birds make up the cast of fauna common to this area. The gleaming trunks of aspen and birch by the big lake are replaced by the upland hardwoods of sugar maple, yellow birch, basswood, and spruce as that mature forest evolves throughout the inland lake country. Scattered throughout the park are frequent lone pines towering above this forest canopy.

RATINGS

Beauty: ☆ ☆ ☆ ☆
Privacy: ☆ ☆ ☆ ☆ ☆
Spaciousness: ☆ ☆ ☆ ☆ ☆
Quiet: ☆ ☆ ☆ ☆
Security: ☆ ☆ ☆
Cleanliness: ☆ ☆ ☆ ☆

The drive-in campground offers some fantastic sites, including probably the nicest one I found in all the state parks visited. Sites 1 through 5 are typical, having all the standard features. They are well screened but small and fairly close to the road compared to others in this area.

The walk-in sites, 6 through 8, are easily accessible from the small parking area at the trail's head. Site 6 sits in a stand of old-growth birch and is very private. Site 7 is located on a slight rise in the forest floor, and 8 is on top of a modest ridge with a growing understory of aspen and balsam fir. There is about 150 feet between sites 7 and 8.

Site 9 is a small, tidy site. Sites 10 through 16 are basic sites within a dense understory. Sites 13 and 14 are partially surrounded by a grove of cedars. Site 15 sits on the edge of a ridge, and 16 sits in a stand of aspen and fir—a quaint site. Sites on either side of the road throughout this loop are all pleasant, inviting camping spots.

Site 18 is probably the smallest site in the loop. A trail heads off to the river, leading down the slope from the road at a point between sites 17 and 20. Site 21 is long and narrow, not much tent space there.

Sites 24 and 25 are walk-in sites, requiring a short hike from the parking area across the road. Site 25 is a spot to cherish. It's not anywhere near the water but is so private and spacious that it's worth extra effort to secure it. Both sites are far enough off the road to give them a true backcountry feel. They are surrounded by clusters of birch, boulders, and a quiet forest. Site 25 has a sprinkling of cedar trees. It is a very private site right off the picnic table and guarded by a towering white pine.

A rock outcropping as the loop starts to circle back on itself is an impressive backdrop to sites 26 and 27. The next few sites are standard and noticeably exposed compared to earlier sites in the loop. The remaining sites vary in size and shape but still retain the character of this campground.

One can imagine these hills aglow in the fall when all the birch and aspen leaves turn their brilliant yellow. Add the reds and oranges of the other hardwoods

KEY INFORMATION

ADDRESS:	5702 MN 61 East Silver Bay, MN 55614
OPERATED BY:	Minnesota DNR, Division of Parks and Recreation
INFORMATION:	(218) 226-6365
OPEN:	Year-round
SITES:	34 semimodern sites, 13 cart-in sites
ASSIGNMENT:	First come, first served, unless reserved
REGISTRATION:	Available at (866) 85-PARKS (72757), or online at www.stay atmnparks.com
FACILITIES:	Restroom, showers, toilet, water, boat ramp
PARKING:	Throughout campground
FEES:	$7 daily permit, $5 group, $25 annual; camping fee $15 semimodern, $18 electric hookup, $11 rustic, $8.50 nonrefundable reservation fee
ACTIVITIES:	More than 23 miles of trails; 5 picnic areas; fishing; 4 waterfall sites
RESTRICTIONS:	**Pets:** On 6-foot maximum leash **Fires:** In designated rings only **Alcohol:** Not allowed **Vehicles:** On designated trails or roads **Other:** Closed to nonregistered campers 10 p.m.– 8 a.m.; use of weapons prohibited; no removal of flora or fauna from park

MAP

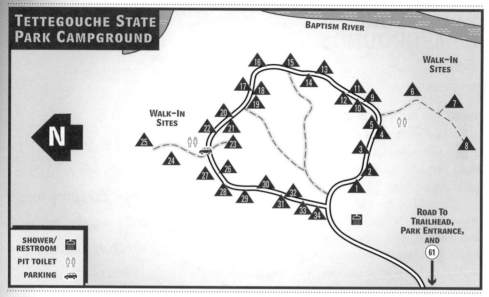

TETTEGOUCHE STATE PARK CAMPGROUND

BAPTISM RIVER

WALK-IN SITES

WALK-IN SITES

N

16 15 13
17 18 14 11 6 7
19 12 10 9
20 5
22 21 8
25 23 4
24 26 3
27 2
28 30 32 1
29 31 33 34

ROAD TO TRAILHEAD, PARK ENTRANCE, AND
61

SHOWER/RESTROOM
PIT TOILET
PARKING

GETTING THERE

From Silver Bay, go north 4.5 miles on MN 61 to the park entrance on the right.

and you can count on excellent fall colors throughout this area.

It's safe to say that if you had only one chance to experience a drive-in tent-camping experience along the North Shore, Tettegouche State Park would be a most gratifying and fulfilling choice!

ZIPPEL BAY
STATE PARK
CAMPGROUNDS

THIS PARK TOOK ME completely by surprise! I am no stranger to northern Minnesota. One of my most enjoyable camping trips ever was on a small island on the Lake of the Woods. But I was not prepared for Zippel Bay State Park.

Located on the southern shore of Lake of the Woods, this is Minnesota's most northern state park. It is situated along a two-mile stretch of beach in a birch and jack pine forest overlooking the oceanic vastness of Lake of the Woods. The lake itself is an awesome body of water, nearly 1,500 square miles with almost 10 times as many islands throughout its waterways. Stand on the banks of Zippel Bay and look to the north—your eyes can't see across the 55 miles of water.

I was at Zippel about a week past the full flush of fall colors. Even then, the golden canopy of birch leaves was almost blinding. Brilliant golden-yellow leaves at the end of long, limber, powdery white tree trunks played beautifully against the blue sky overhead. Fantastic fall coloration greeted me throughout the park. The birch stands in some areas were so thick, so tightly grown, their long gleaming white trunks so close together, that I made an entry in my notebook that reads: "I feel like a flea on the back of a white-haired dog!" Amid this wash of whites and yellows, the campgrounds are laid out.

There are four campgrounds at Zippel Bay: Lady's Slipper, Birch, Ridge, and Anglers. Lady's Slipper has the fewest sites, all off one long driveway ending in a cul-de-sac. The 11 sites alternate on each side of the road. The sites are nestled into the woods, but the lack of understory and space between sites does not afford much privacy.

Birch campground is anchored in a thick sea of birch. The campground is at the end of a 200-yard

> *This fisherman's park is set into a thicket of picturesque birch trees on the southern shore of Lake of the Woods.*

RATINGS

Beauty: ✿ ✿ ✿
Privacy: ✿ ✿ ✿
Spaciousness: ✿ ✿ ✿
Quiet: ✿ ✿ ✿
Security: ✿ ✿ ✿ ✿
Cleanliness: ✿ ✿ ✿ ✿

ADDRESS: 3684 54th Avenue NW
Williams, MN 56686

OPERATED BY: Minnesota DNR, Division of Parks and Recreation

INFORMATION: (218) 783-6252

OPEN: Year-round

SITES: 60 drive-in sites

ASSIGNMENT: First come, first served, unless reserved

REGISTRATION: Available at (866) 85-PARKS (72757), or online at www.stay atmnparks.com

FACILITIES: Drinking water, toilet, RV sanitation station, shower

PARKING: On right just before entering campground

FEES: $7 daily permit, $5 group, $25 annual permit; camping fee $15 semimodern, $18 electric hookup, $11 rustic; $8.50 nonrefundable reservation fee

ACTIVITIES: Fishing, public boat harbor, launching ramp and dock, picnic and fish-cleaning areas, hiking

RESTRICTIONS: Pets: On 6-foot maximum leash
Fires: In designated rings only
Alcohol: Not allowed
Vehicles: On designated trails or roads
Other: Closed to nonregistered campers 10 p.m.–8 a.m.; use of weapons prohibited; no removal of flora or fauna from park

spur off the main road. Sites 2 through 17 are fairly close together. Sites begin to spread out a bit more at 18. All the sites in Birch, Ridge, and Angler are outside the camping road loop, so there are no sites directly or alternately across from each other. Sites at the tip of the loop are the most private and spacious.

Ridge is probably the best campground of the four as far as space between sites and a general sense of privacy, sitting at the end of a long, narrow lane—farther than depicted on the park map. Sites on the northern and southern edges of the loop are a bit farther apart (29 through 32, and 37 through 40).

Angler's campground is, as the name implies, a convenient campsite for those heavily into boat fishing. Angler's is closest to the marina area, and each site is large enough to accommodate a large tent, vehicles, and presumably boat trailers. There is not much of an understory at Angler's, but the birch and interspersed jack pine give it a wonderful, woodsy setting.

Besides the dominance of birch trees throughout the park, expect to see clusters of aspen (abnormally whitish bark) inland, gradually changing to birch closer to the lake. There are patches of evergreens in the park, too, namely balsam fir, in the area around Angler's campground. Jack pines are scattered throughout the park as well, but it's clearly the white paper birch that catch and hold the eye.

The park's list of natural amenities is mighty impressive. There are four species of lady's slippers and several other orchid species. Wild berries—blue, June, cran, and straw—abound in June and July, as do mushrooms, pin cherries, and choke cherries.

Wildlife-viewing possibilities abound as well: coyote, black bear, mink, fisher, otter, and even a rare pine martin. Even timberwolves are seen or heard in the park. Deer and an occasional moose are seen as well.

Birding is a popular activity in the park, as many species are attracted to the great expanse of water and its miles of shoreline! White pelicans, double-crested cormorants, several gull varieties, and four species of terns are common along the park's shoreline. Less common sandhill cranes frequent a marsh just north of Zippel Bay. You might even see the endangered piping

MAP

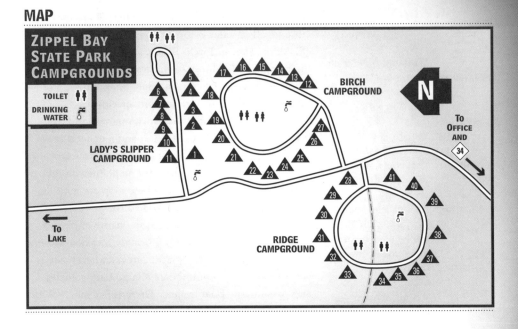

ZIPPEL BAY
STATE PARK
CAMPGROUNDS

TOILET

DRINKING
WATER

LADY'S SLIPPER
CAMPGROUND

BIRCH
CAMPGROUND

N

To
OFFICE
AND
34

To
LAKE

RIDGE
CAMPGROUND

plover; Lake of the Woods is the largest breeding ground for this species of only 50 known breeding pairs.

Historically, this park has been the resident grounds for several Native American tribes. French explorers scouted out this area in the early 1700s. By the late 1880s a small fishing village was established by the park's namesake, William M. Zippel.

The big draw of Zippel Bay is, of course, Lake of the Woods—a most impressive body of water. Fishing for walleye is the most popular activity on the lake (with a sauger or two taken, and even a sturgeon), with beachcombing and swimming at the park a close second and third. Still, in my view, the park is worth a camping outing for the birch forests alone.

GETTING THERE

From Williams, go about 6 miles east on CR 13 to CR 4, turn left (north) and go about 6 miles to CR 8. Turn left (west) and drive about 1 mile to CR 34, then turn right (north) on CR 34 to the park entrance.

MAP

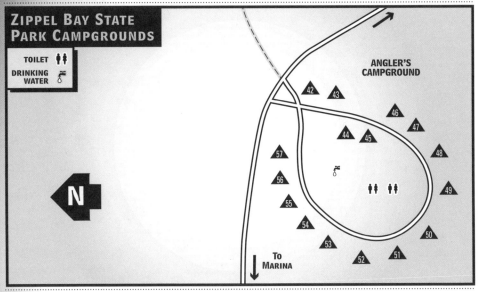

ZIPPEL BAY STATE
PARK CAMPGROUNDS

TOILET
DRINKING
WATER

ANGLER'S
CAMPGROUND

42 43

46
47
44 45
48
57
56
55
49
54
50
53
51
52

N

To
MARINA

CENTRAL MINNESOTA

ANN LAKE CAMPGROUND

IT'S RARE THAT I would recommend camping in an area shared by horseback riding, but Ann Lake, with offerings for both horseback riders and snowmobilers, is also a pretty darn good place to camp and hike. Besides, those other two popular activities are not allowed in the camping area designated on maps as the Bob Dunn Recreation Area.

If you've only camped or visited state parks, state forests offer a new way of enjoying and appreciating the outdoors. In some ways, state forests seem less structured and less developed—but they are by no means less appealing. The recreational opportunities in Minnesota's forests are less structured—back to the basics of hunting, fishing, and just plain enjoying the outdoors. You will be ahead of the game if you are easily entertained by nature itself. A state forest setting may not always be as spectacular as a state park or have nearly the geological, historical, or other amenities that single them out from the outdoors in general. Yet state forest campgrounds are a pleasant way to enjoy the forest for what it is—either in passing through on an overnight, or as the final destination for a week's stay under the stars.

What I especially like about the state forest campgrounds is that they are usually located off the main arteries of highways and scenic routes and often are stuck in the middle of nowhere—even within the forest itself. They are basic campsites cut out of the forest and developed, to the extent that there is a tent site, picnic table, fire ring, pit toilet, and other amenities. "Wait a minute," you are probably saying, "that's as much as a state park offers?" Yes, indeed, basic sites with all the basic needs in a more utilitarian setting—but wonderful camping just the same.

That said, here's what's special about Ann Lake. First of all, it is situated within Sand Dunes State Forest.

> *Ann Lake features pine- and oak-covered sand dunes laced with rambling trails.*

RATINGS

Beauty: ✩ ✩ ✩
Privacy: ✩ ✩ ✩
Spaciousness: ✩ ✩ ✩
Quiet: ✩ ✩ ✩
Security: ✩ ✩ ✩
Cleanliness: ✩ ✩ ✩

ADDRESS: Area Forester
Department of
Natural Resources
800 Oak Savanna
Lane SW
Cambridge, MN
55008

OPERATED BY: Minnesota DNR,
Division of Forestry,
(651) 296-6157

INFORMATION: (763) 878-2325

OPEN: Year-round

SITES: 36 drive-in; 6 walk-in

ASSIGNMENT: First come, first
served; reservations
for group sites only

REGISTRATION: Not available

FACILITIES: Restrooms, vault
toilets, water, boat
ramp nearby

PARKING: At both ends of the
trail loop into the
walk-in sites

FEES: $10 per night; group
site $30 per night or
$2/person,
whichever is greater

ACTIVITIES: Horseback riding
trails, snowmobile
and hiking trails,
swimming, boat
ramp

RESTRICTIONS: **Pets:** On leash
Fires: Must be in
cleared areas at least
5 feet around, and
built less than 3 feet
in diameter
Alcohol: Not allowed
Vehicles: No motor-
ized vehicles on non-
motorized trails
Other: Hunting and
firearms only in
posted areas;
camping possible in
undeveloped areas

This area used to be part of the expansive prairie system that covered the western and southwestern parts of Minnesota. However, the sandy soils were not conducive to pioneer farming methods, and those who homesteaded this region fought long and hard to grow crops here. During the Great Depression, it was determined that that area's economy could be better established if trees were planted in the sandy soil. Since the early 1940s, more than 2,400 acres of tree plantations have been established in this area. Many of the hiking trails throughout the Bob Dunn Recreation Area pass through these blocks of plantings. The forests in and around Ann Lake were eventually built up to cover more than 17 square miles, featuring northern pines as well as other species (predominantly oak) that found the area suitable for growth.

You can't help but notice the stands of red pine and oak varieties within this campground. Each site offers a spacious setting under a bur oak canopy. Sites 3 through 13 are set into a hilly oak-forested area with an ample understory that suggests a bit of privacy and quietness.

The next few sites, 14 through 21, are much closer together but are laid out to provide ample room within each site's immediate area. Generally the sites are well spread out among the hills and the turns of the campground road to create individual campsites— either on knolls or in openings scattered throughout the woods. The entire lower campground loop offers a thick understory giving each site a sense of isolation from the rest.

Sites 8 through 14 are situated on higher, more open ground. These sites appear to be less private but have a more commanding view and presence within the campground's first loop.

The lower end of the 2-mile nature trail can be accessed at the entrance to the campground. A short trail takes hikers to a fork that lets them access the Red Loop in either direction for a full round of hiking through pine plantations and stands of oaks and along ridgelines atop the dunes.

The walk-in sites are located at the end of the main campground loop. As in all the other areas covered in this book, the walk-in sites are usually my

MAP

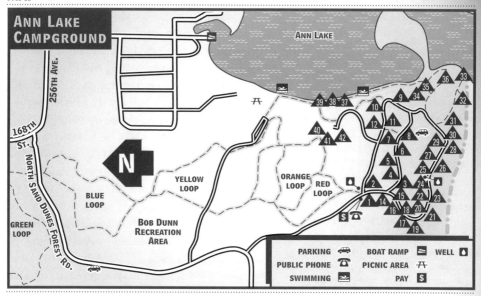

ANN LAKE CAMPGROUND

ANN LAKE

256TH AVE.

168TH ST.

NORTH SAND DUNES FOREST RD.

N

YELLOW LOOP

BLUE LOOP

GREEN LOOP

BOB DUNN RECREATION AREA

ORANGE LOOP

RED LOOP

PARKING	🚐	BOAT RAMP	⊟	WELL	◘
PUBLIC PHONE	☎	PICNIC AREA	ㅈ		
SWIMMING	🏊	PAY	$		

favorite picks. I love the solitude and the basic amenities. These sites are nestled among the knolls or dunes
of the park. Campsites 35 and 36 overlook Ann Lake.

The best campsites are in the group camp area
just below the fire tower and immediately above the
lake. It's a beautiful setting in the shadow of the old
fire tower and a planting of white pines started in 1978.
There is a spur from the main trail system that leads
into this camping area. It connects with the Orange
Loop on the trail system, which then intersects with
other loops in the network.

I found the group site to be the most beautiful in
the park. Gather up a half dozen or so of those you'd
most like to camp with and make a reservation for the
group site—I doubt you'll be disappointed.

Note: If you enjoy bird-watching, the northern section of the Sherburne National Wildlife Refuge is a
mere 6-mile drive north of Ann Lake. It features a 7-
mile wildlife drive through grasslands, along a series of
drainage gates, and through controlled sloughs for fantastic waterfowl and shorebird watching. The loop is a
great hiking trail, too. There are also several opportunities to see nesting bald eagles!

GETTING THERE

From Zimmerman,
take CR 4 west 6 miles to
168th Street (North Sand
Dunes Forest Road), turn left
(south), and follow the signs
1.5 miles to State Forest
Road 171, turn left, and go
(southeast) 0.3 mile to the fee
box at the campground.

BANNING STATE PARK CAMPGROUND

> *Geological offerings abound in this park dominated by the Kettle River—it's truly a treasure chest of natural amenities.*

ALTHOUGH THIS PARK is teeming with amenities such as a waterfall, sets of rapids, exposed bedrock, and all the other natural features of the great northern Minnesota woods, it doesn't, at first drive-through, appear to have a striking landscape or stunning vistas—at least the areas I was able to visit. Clearly, however, its geological features are sights worth seeing and make it a park worth visiting for those treasures alone.

Banning State Park is comprised of over 6,200 acres adjacent to the Kettle River, one of Minnesota's Wild and Scenic Waterways. Cutting through the bedrock that underlies most of Minnesota and is exposed throughout so much of the north country, Banning's Kettle River has carved out several sets of rapids as it courses through the park. If you are not a river runner, you can at least enjoy an afternoon of watching the more courageous river rats shooting these disturbances.

One section of the river, Hell's Gate, is a graphic example of the geological forces that have sculpted this park. After carving a trough through 100 feet of Precambrian sandstone, the Kettle River carved sheer, 40-foot cliffs out of the bedrock to create this canyon.

More fanciful geological formations within the park include the Bat Cave (Robinson's Ice Cave), the "kettles," Log Creek arches, sandstone quarry, and Wolf Creek Falls.

This is a birder's park, featuring over 184 species of birds that either visit or migrate through the park. Other wildlife abounds, offering visitors a long list of critters to see during a visit.

Human influences in the park can be seen mostly from the aspen and birch trees that dominate the forest. These are what came in to replace all the white and red pine harvested during Minnesota's logging

RATINGS

Beauty: ✩ ✩
Privacy: ✩ ✩
Spaciousness: ✩ ✩ ✩
Quiet: ✩ ✩ ✩
Security: ✩ ✩ ✩
Cleanliness: ✩ ✩ ✩

blitt. A few towering pines and an understory that includes younger spruce indicate that the forest is slowly maturing.

This area was devastated by the great Hinckley forest fire of 1894. Banning, named after the president of the local railroad, saw its population decline after several more forest fires in the area and was abandoned by 1912.

Camping in Banning State Park is confined to one three-section loop located in the center of the long, narrow, north–south-oriented park. Most of the trail systems pass between the camping area and the river just east of the campground.

The first section of the loop contains eight sites, five of which include electricity and so will attract the RVs and appliance-dependent campers. It's a small lane with red pine, aspen, and paper birch. Sites 1 through 3 are surrounded by a good screening from the abundant understory—pretty basic sites otherwise.

Sites 9 through 17 are off staggered driveways, which means a modest degree of privacy as far as looking across the road to another site. However, these sites are fairly well exposed to the road down the driveway. A thick understory increases privacy, and probably helps muffle the sound a bit, too. Sites 10, 11, and 12 all offer electrical hookups.

The last section of the loop contains sites 18 through 34; these are the better sites for optimum tent-camping enjoyment. The inner sites, 20, 22, and 24, also are electrically enhanced. This section is within a stand of older aspen, and many sites have a dense understory to promote privacy and quiet.

Site 18 has a long driveway off the main loop and backs up to the forest. It is very isolated and private. Site 19, also on the outer edge of the loop is nestled into that dense understory. Actually, even those sites within the loop are adequately spaced to offer a sense of privacy. Site 23, on the other hand, is too open for my liking. Sites 24 and 25 are good sites size-wise but are also more open than the former sites in this loop. The only rental cabin in the park is located right next to site 29, across from site 30. Site 32, although in the inner loop, is a very big site but lacks understory.

KEY INFORMATION

ADDRESS: P.O. Box 643 Sandstone, MN 55072

OPERATED BY: Minnesota DNR, Division of Parks and Recreation

INFORMATION: (320) 245-2668

OPEN: Year-round

SITES: 33 semi-modern, 4 canoe sites, 1 cabin

ASSIGNMENT: First come, first served, unless reserved

REGISTRATION: At (866) 85-PARKS (72757), or online at www.stayatmn parks.com

FACILITIES: Restroom, showers, recycling center, electrical sites, water

PARKING: Past entrance to campground loop

FEES: $7 daily permit, $5 group, $25 annual; camping fee $15 semimodern, $18 electric hookup, $11 rustic, $8.50 nonrefundable reservation fee

ACTIVITIES: Bird-watching, 14 miles of hiking trails, 11 miles of skiing trails, canoeing, kayaking, fishing

RESTRICTIONS: Pets: On 6-foot maximum leash Fires: In designated rings only Alcohol: Not allowed Vehicles: On designated trails or roads Other: Closed to nonregistered campers 10 p.m.– 8 a.m.; no removal of flora or fauna from park

MAP

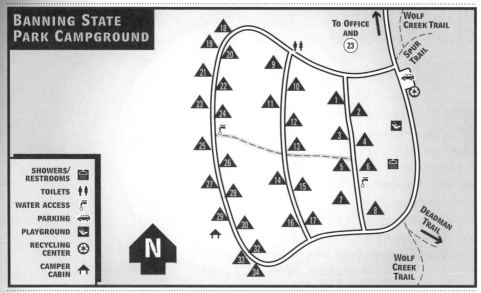

BANNING STATE PARK CAMPGROUND

To Office AND (23)

WOLF CREEK TRAIL

SPUR TRAIL

DEADMAN TRAIL

WOLF CREEK TRAIL

SHOWERS/RESTROOMS
TOILETS
WATER ACCESS
PARKING
PLAYGROUND
RECYCLING CENTER
CAMPER CABIN

N

GETTING THERE

From Sandstone go north 4 miles on MN 23 to the campground entrance, or stay on I-35 and take exit #195 to the park entrance 4 miles north of Sandstone.

This area features stands of aspens intermixed with evergreens (mostlyspruce and balsam fir) creating a pleasant contrast of colors that is certainly heightened during peak fall colors when the deep green of the spruce is the backdrop for the brilliant gold colors of the aspen.

Banning State Park's forest floor is covered with barrel-sized boulders—remnants of the tremendous geological influences on this region of Minnesota. For those who enjoy learning and seeing all evidence of Minnesota's rich geological history, Banning should be just the spot. Bird-watchers and hikers will be equally rewarded.

BUNKER HILLS RUSTIC LOOP CAMPGROUND

BUNKER HILLS REGIONAL PARK lies just beyond the last of the suburbs of the metropolitan Twin Cities, north side (including the Anoka area), and the ever-expanding open country to the north. Bunker Hills is a pocket of sandy hills, oak forests, and a small lake that has been developed into one of the major regional parks in Anoka County. This park is probably more renowned for its incredible water park that draws swimmers, waders, and splashers from all around the seven-county metro area. I doubt many people even realize it has a campground—and a choice one at that!

Like the campsite listed for Cleary Lake (see page 145), Bunker Lake campground is in a regional park and as such is part of a complex of recreational activities that also includes a golf course and a water park. Hiking trails wind through the campground and wooded areas; riding stables are located within the park, and the local lake offers boating and fishing. The programs and amenities are all designed for and openly encourage full family participation and enjoyment.

There is a wonderful walking/biking trail that works its way through the Bunker Hill complex. It curves through the oaks and up and over swales along its wooded course. The total trail is about 5 miles long and at several points intersects with spurs that offer shortcuts back to the campgrounds or to some of the key recreational sections of the park (the water park, for example). Bird-watchers will be kept busy with all the park's songbirds.

There are two campground loops at Bunker Hills, completely serviced with hookups for RVs, and one rustic loop for tent camping. The Rustic Loop features 23 campsites spread out among a cluster of oaks and pine trees, offering large sites with

> *This rustic oak-forest setting is just minutes north of downtown Minneapolis and has a true country-camping atmosphere.*

RATINGS

Beauty: ☆ ☆ ☆
Privacy: ☆ ☆ ☆ ☆
Spaciousness: ☆ ☆ ☆ ☆
Quiet: ☆ ☆ ☆
Security: ☆ ☆ ☆ ☆
Cleanliness: ☆ ☆ ☆ ☆

ADDRESS: Activities Center
Building
550 Bunker Lake
Boulevard NW
Andover, MN 55304

OPERATED BY: Bunker Hills
Regional Park,
Anoka County Parks
and Recreation

INFORMATION: (763) 862-4970

OPEN: May–mid-October

SITES: 23 rustic campsites

ASSIGNMENT: First come, first
served, unless
reserved

REGISTRATION: At campground
office; reserve sites
for $3 at (763) 862-
4970, 7 days a week

FACILITIES: Restroom and showers, water, pay phone

PARKING: At individual sites

FEES: $5 daily permit, $25
annual; camping fee
$15 rustic site

ACTIVITIES: Hiking, swimming
and water park,
horseback riding,
golf, picnic area

RESTRICTIONS: **Pets:** On a leash and
attended at all times
Fires: In rings only,
collecting of fire-
wood not allowed
Alcohol: Beer only
Vehicles: No parking
on grass; all vehicles
must have an Anoka
or Washington
County Vehicle Per-
mit on windshield
Other: Check in/out
1 p.m.; 10 people
and 2 camping units
maximum per site;
Quiet hours 10 p.m.–
7 a.m.; fireworks not
allowed

optimum privacy in most cases.

Because this is a continuation of the campground numbering system that includes the RV side, the Rustic Loop begins at site 25. It is a fairly exposed site-backed by red pines and oaks. Likewise, site 26 is exposed and is adjacent to a small playground area. The road through the campground twists through a forest of oak trees, both mature trees that form the canopy overhead and saplings that make up the under-story. There are a few aspens intermixed—like those scattered around site 27, which sits on a rise above the roadway.

Site 28 is open and grassy, and the site directly across the road, 29, sits in a grove of trees. Both are screened by a dense understory. Site 30 is off the road to the right in a little pocket of large oaks all by itself. The road continues through the trees, but off to the right you'll get a glimpse of the water park area. In the summer, expect to hear it way before you see it.

Sites 31, 32, and 33 are all exposed to the road but are within defined open areas, making them uncrowded places to pitch a tent. These sites all have large, looming oak trees standing sentinel over the site.

Site 34 is divided up into four sites, A, B, C, and D at the end of a short spur off the main campground road. Each site has a short access trail leading to it before it opens into a clearing in the woods. These are shaded sites, off the main trail; they are especially pleasant spots.

Site 35 sits up on a grassy knoll surrounded by gnarly oak trees. Site 36 is exposed to the road a bit more than others but is back far enough in the trees to provide a private, grassy area for pitching a tent or two. Sites 37 through 39 are fairly open, grassy sites; 38 is amid clusters of smaller oaks, and 39 is near a hiking trail intersection.

Sites 40 to 44 seemed the least private, most exposed sites in the park, mainly because the entrance road to the campground runs behind them (except for site 42) and can be seen through the trees.

Bunker Hills is a cross between the nearby north-woods and the oak savannahs of south-central and eastern Minnesota. It's got charm, class, and lots of

MAP

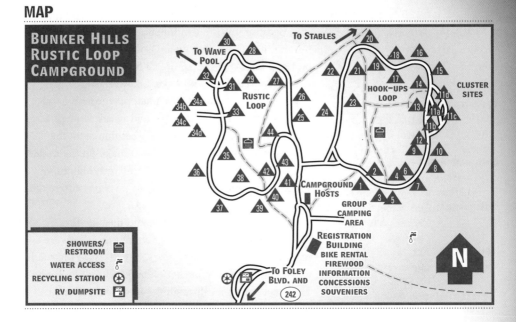

BUNKER HILLS RUSTIC LOOP CAMPGROUND

TO STABLES

TO WAVE POOL

RUSTIC LOOP

HOOK-UPS LOOP

CLUSTER SITES

CAMPGROUND HOSTS

GROUP CAMPING AREA

REGISTRATION BUILDING
BIKE RENTAL
FIREWOOD
INFORMATION
CONCESSIONS
SOUVENIERS

TO FOLEY BLVD. AND 242

SHOWERS/ RESTROOM	
WATER ACCESS	
RECYCLING STATION	
RV DUMPSITE	

N

spacious campsites that put many state park campgrounds to shame. Its proximity to the Twin Cities makes it an good pick for weekend camping trips when you just need to get out of the house for a while. Be sure to take the Rustic Loop, otherwise you'll be in the ring of wagons at the RV campground.

GETTING THERE

From Minneapolis take I-35W north to US 10; go west to MN 65. At MN 65 take a right (north) and go 8 miles to MN 242. Turn left (west) and go 3 miles to the entrance at Foley Boulevard. Turn right (north) into park. From St. Paul take I-35E north to I-694 west. Go west on I-694 about 6 miles to I-35W and then follow the directions above.

FATHER HENNEPIN STATE PARK CAMPGROUND

> *This quaint, unimposing park is situated in a lush stand of maples on the southern shore of Mille Lacs Lake.*

I AM NOT A FREQUENT VISITOR to the Mille Lacs Lake area. I am usually in a hurry to get farther north to spend the weekend camping and then head back home. In all the years of doing just that, I have been driving right by a site that offers the quaintness of many of the parks I'd ventured farther out for. That said, I must admit that Father Hennepin's camping, though not spectacular, is pleasant, feels homey, and offers campers an opportunity to enjoy a woodsy feeling on the otherwise continually developed shoreline of one of Minnesota's more popular fishing lakes.

There are two main campgrounds at Father Hennepin, both a short jaunt from the lake. Lakeview is the larger of the two and could be called "parking lot camping"—this is where the RVs go to camp. 'Nuff said.

Maple Grove Campground features one of the most distinguishing characteristics of this park—its dense stand of maples: sugar, red, and all the standard northern varieties. When intermixed with red oaks, these forests become especially beautiful. They flame with yellows and reds in the fall—one more reason for keeping this little gem on your short list of parks to visit.

Each camping area is separated by these woods, which also include a scattering of spruce and birch between uncommonly long and narrow sites. Camping along the outer loop provides more privacy than sites within the circles. Some tents end up back to back within the inner network of drives that separate one section from another.

If I were to reserve a campsite at Maple Grove, I'd opt for sites 92 to 94. They are on the outer edge of the loop and feature all the amenities common to a state park: tent site, picnic table, and fire ring. If this still doesn't really excite you, just wait—there's one

RATINGS

Beauty: ✰ ✰ ✰
Privacy: ✰ ✰ ✰ ✰
Spaciousness: ✰ ✰ ✰
Quiet: ✰ ✰ ✰
Security: ✰ ✰ ✰
Cleanliness: ✰ ✰ ✰ ✰

more place to pitch a tent among the trees of Father Hennepin.

Shown on the park's map as a cluster of individual sites located near the group camp, the walk-in sites barely qualify as such because you can drive up to within about 20 feet of the nearest campsite. Each site has a cart to make hauling your gear easier.

These sites are actually nestled within a stand of birch. Sites 3 through 6 are off to the right from the parking lot and far enough away that you might hear more boisterous neighbors but probably won't see them. Site 2 is close at hand right off the parking lot. A couple of pit toilets near sites 1 and 2, and a water pump at the corner of the parking lot are the extent of facilities you'll find here. Any of these are clearly my picks for the best sites in this park.

All campgrounds are connected by a trail system, part of the 4-mile network within the park. Nearly half of those pathways are along Mille Lacs Lake—from the information office at the park's entrance to the long stretch along the shore to the other end of the trail at Pope Point. Combination hike/ski trails also loop throughout the forested area to the west of the primitive sites for another couple of miles of forested trekking.

Because of the park's diverse vegetation, grasslands, and mixed softwoods, wildlife abounds: hawks, osprey, deer, beaver, raccoon, and a host of birds make their homes within the woods, ponds, and along the lakeshore.

Mille Lacs is the second largest lake within Minnesota's boundaries and is renowned for its excellent fishing, especially walleye. Visitors to the park can try their angling prowess at the fishing pier or from any point along the shore. There are scores of charter operations in nearby towns from which to reserve a fishing trip on the lake.

Clearly the more casual and less developed of the two state parks on the lake (Mille Lacs Kathio State Park is about 15 miles to the west), Father Hennepin offers the same natural amenities but on a smaller and less developed scale. For a near-north camping experience on one of Minnesota's busiest lakes, plan at least a stopover visit to this park.

KEY INFORMATION

ADDRESS: P.O. Box 397 Isle, MN 56342

OPERATED BY: Minnesota DNR, Division of Parks and Recreation

INFORMATION: (320) 676-8763

OPEN: Year-round

SITES: 103 semimodern; 5 primitive sites

ASSIGNMENT: First come, first served, unless reserved

REGISTRATION: Available by calling (866) 85-PARKS (72757), or reserve online at www.stay atmnparks.com

FACILITIES: Restrooms, vault toilets, water, trailer sanitation station

PARKING: At entrance to center loop of each campsite and at hub of trails at walk-in site

FEES: $7 daily permit, $5 group, $25 annual; camping fee $15 semimodern, $18 electric hookup, $11 rustic; $8.50 nonrefundable reservation fee

ACTIVITIES: Swimming, fishing, hiking, boating

RESTRICTIONS: Pets: On 6-foot maximum leash Fires: In designated rings only Alcohol: Not allowed Vehicles: On designated trails or roads Other: Closed to nonregistered campers 10 p.m.–8 a.m.; use of weapons prohibited; no removal of flora or fauna from park

MAP

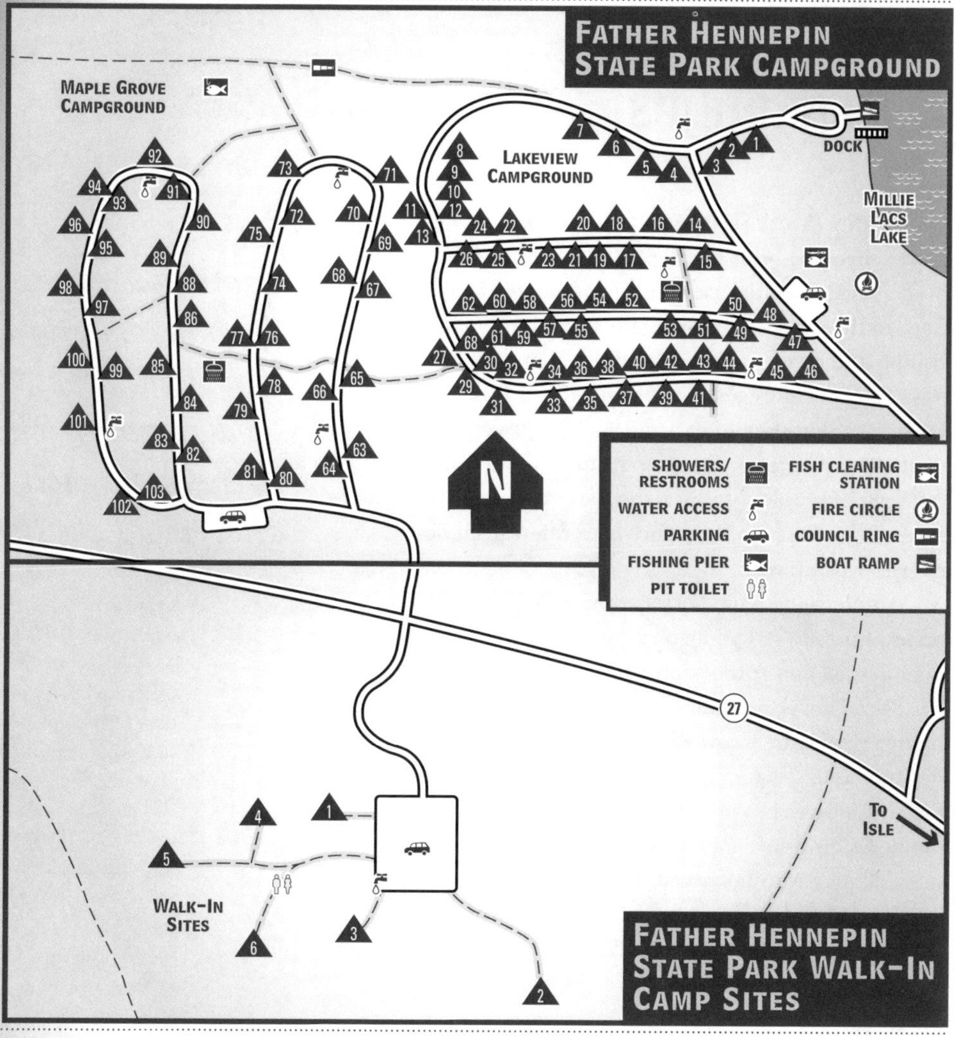

FATHER HENNEPIN STATE PARK CAMPGROUND

MAPLE GROVE CAMPGROUND

LAKEVIEW CAMPGROUND

DOCK

MILLE LACS LAKE

N

SHOWERS/RESTROOMS	FISH CLEANING STATION
WATER ACCESS	FIRE CIRCLE
PARKING	COUNCIL RING
FISHING PIER	BOAT RAMP
PIT TOILET	

27

TO ISLE

WALK-IN SITES

FATHER HENNEPIN STATE PARK WALK-IN CAMP SITES

GETTING THERE

Turn north into the park entrance on MN 27, 1 mile west of the town of Isle.

HUNTERSVILLE/ SHELL CITY STATE FOREST CAMPGROUNDS

THIS IS A "TWO-FER" campsite reference because both Huntersville and Shell City provide a similar camping experience. They are both in the same state forest, on small rivers ideal for fishing and canoeing, and are modest in their facilities. They are only a short distance from Itasca State Park, meaning they offer a more modest, yet adequate, alternative to the campgrounds at the bigger state park complex. In fact, they are managed by Itasca State Park, so they may be a referral site for overflow camping.

Huntersville State Forest comprises 52 square miles of mostly red and jack pine forests with a scattering of aspen and spruce and a variety of northern hardwood covering rolling, sandy hills. The area is cut by two rivers, the Crow Wing and the Shell. Like most of Minnesota's state forests, this one is managed for its forest resources but provides some recreational opportunities. Campsites are typically at water's edge—the main activity is usually boating and fishing.

The Shell River campsite is adjacent to a horse camp whose campers can use 22 miles of horse trails. In the winter, snowmobilers race along 15 miles of dedicated trails. Hikers should find plenty of places to trek using the 150-plus miles of logging trails throughout the forest. These routes are shared by hikers, bikers, and drivers.

The big attraction at these two campsites is the river flowing past each campground. Both the Shell and the Crow River provide many canoeing opportunities, with access ramps at the these campgrounds as well as other put-in and take-out points along the river's course through the forest. These are accessed by landing turnouts along county roads in the area. This boating route winds along 80 miles of river and offers a wilderness campsite every 3 to 7 miles. The Shell

> *Quaint and somewhat Spartan campsites, each on the banks of small, northern forest rivers—just a short drive from Lake Itasca.*

RATINGS

Beauty: ✩ ✩ ✩
Privacy: ✩ ✩ ✩
Spaciousness: ✩ ✩ ✩
Quiet: ✩ ✩ ✩
Security: ✩ ✩ ✩
Cleanliness: ✩ ✩ ✩

KEY INFORMATION

ADDRESS: Area Forest Supervisor Department of Natural Resources Box 6 Backus, MN 56435

OPERATED BY: Minnesota DNR, Division of Forestry

INFORMATION: (218) 472-3262 (both sites managed by Itasca State Park)

OPEN: Year-round

SITES: 17 drive-in, 7 walk-in at Huntersville; 19 sites at Shell City

ASSIGNMENT: First come, first served

REGISTRATION: Group camps only

FACILITIES: Vault toilets, boat ramp, well water only at Huntersville

PARKING: At boat landing

FEES: $10 per night; group site $30 per night or $2 per person, whichever is greater

ACTIVITIES: Horseback-riding trails, snowmobile and hiking trails, swimming, boat ramp on Ann Lake

RESTRICTIONS: Pets: On leash only Fires: In cleared area at least 5 feet around and built less than 3 feet in diameter Alcohol: Not allowed Vehicles: No motorized vehicles on any nonmotorized trails or in posted areas that prohibit use Other: Hunting and firearms only in posted areas; camping possible in undeveloped areas (special rules apply)

flows into the Crow Wing River a few miles east of the Shell City campground.

The campground at Huntersville looks more like a picnic area with tent sites. The best camping is at the group sites, which ensure a spacious site and a better chance at a more private experience. These sites are set in a dense stand of aspen, birch, and maple. Because a large family with at least two or three tents— or a group of friends with as many or more—qualifies as a group, these are definitely the sites to claim! Of the two sites, D4 and D5 are more open and spacious.

The sites at Shell City are more wooded, and there, too, the group sites along the river are nicest. These would be great places for a group of canoeing families to meet for a relaxing weekend both on and off the river. The Shell River is a slow-moving, peaceful stream with lush reeds and rushes growing along its banks. Like the Crow Wing, the Shell is a relatively shallow, sandy-bottomed river (good for swimming) that meanders peacefully through stands of pine. The campground itself is under a towering stand of white pine and close to the road. It's not going to be overly private, but the mood is certainly inviting.

The state forests are managed for their timber, and the recreational amenities are usually minimal unless your camping weekend focus revolves around boating and fishing—or you are able to entertain yourself without programs and interpretive trails. The independent birder/photographer/wildlife viewer will be right at home in these modest campgrounds. If that sounds like you, these two sites are ideal for a casual, low-key weekend or longer camping experience. The self-sufficient canoe-camper will enjoy the paddling routes while the hiker explores all the logging roads.

A word of warning: All the roads in state forest are open to ATVs during the summer months. Be advised, too, that many of the state forest campgrounds are used by horseback riders, either for camping or day use. Trails used by horses tend to get churned up into a fine dust or excessively mired in the rain. Check the campground map—most trails are designated, so be sure to stay off the horse trails and hope those riders do likewise with the hiking-only routes.

MAP

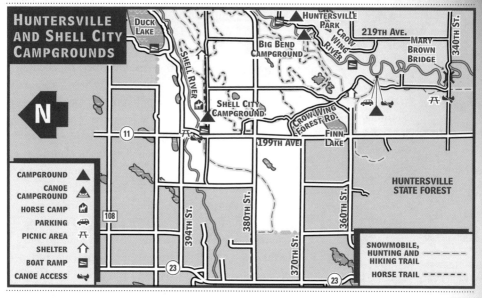

HUNTERSVILLE AND SHELL CITY CAMPGROUNDS

DUCK LAKE

HUNTERSVILLE PARK

BIG BEND CAMPGROUND

219TH AVE.

MARY BROWN BRIDGE

SHELL RIVER

CROW WING RIVER

340TH ST.

SHELL CITY CAMPGROUND

CROW WING FOREST RD.

199TH AVE

FINN LAKE

11

108

HUNTERSVILLE STATE FOREST

N

CAMPGROUND ▲
CANOE CAMPGROUND ▲
HORSE CAMP 🏠
PARKING 🚐
PICNIC AREA 🪑
SHELTER ⇧
BOAT RAMP ◧
CANOE ACCESS 🛶

394TH ST.
380TH ST.
370TH ST.
360TH ST.

23

23

SNOWMOBILE, HUNTING AND HIKING TRAIL ― ― ―
HORSE TRAIL - - - - -

GETTING THERE

Huntersville: From Menahga, take Stocking Lake Road east 4 miles to CR 23, turn left (north), and go 1 mile to 380th Street. Turn right (east) and travel 3 miles to 199th Avenue; turn right (south) and go 1 mile to the sign, turn left and go about 2 miles.

Shell City: From Menahga, take Stocking Lake Road east 4 miles to CR 23, turn left (north), and go 1 mile to 380th Street. Turn right (east) and go 3 miles to 199th Avenue; turn left (north) and travel 1 mile.

JAY COOKE STATE PARK CAMPGROUND

> *Here are some of the most breathtaking waterfalls and cascades in Minnesota, among a vast network of trails overlooking the river.*

EACH TIME I HAVE VISITED Jay Cook State Park, I am awed by the beauty and unrelenting power displayed by the St. Louis River as it continues to literally rip and roar through this park. The magnitude of this mighty river and the stark ruggedness of the rocky channel through which it courses are overpowering. The sounds of the churning water, the mist rising from each cascading drop and chute—all are testament to the natural forces that continue to form the landscape at Jay Cooke State Park.

If you are a hiker, you have your trails cut out for you—over 50 miles' worth! Once you cross the suspension bridge to the southern bank of the river, your choices seem as numerous as the different courses the water takes around and over the rocks. Carlton Trail runs along the southern bank for nearly half the length of the park. Others circle down to the river and up through the higher elevations and distant lakes and shelters. Clearly, one could spend a week hiking all the routes featured on the park map.

The geological history of the park is displayed at every vantage point above the river. Slate, graywacke, and red clay are the dominant deposits and geological features showcased in the park. Ancient mud flats became the shale that, with the graywacke, was exposed during great angular, upward movements of the Earth's crust. Cracks in this upheaved mass were filled in with lava during later geological disturbances. Cooled lava dikes can be seen in the riverbed today. The red clay seen in a widening in the river's gorge is a deposit created by the ancient glacial Lake Duluth that flooded the St. Louis River valley.

Jay Cooke is also noted for its healthy population of Minnesota's larger wildlife residents—deer, black bear, and timber wolf. More than 170 species of birds can be found in the park as well.

RATINGS

Beauty: ✿ ✿ ✿ ✿
Privacy: ✿ ✿ ✿ ✿
Spaciousness: ✿ ✿ ✿ ✿
Quiet: ✿ ✿ ✿ ✿
Security: ✿ ✿ ✿ ✿
Cleanliness: ✿ ✿ ✿ ✿

This part of Minnesota adjacent to the great Lake Superior is also rich in the history of the French fur traders, the voyageurs. Along with Dakota Indian guides, they plied the rivers, traversed the portages, and maintained commercial routes throughout northeastern Minnesota and Canada over 200 years ago.

The campgrounds are right across the highway from the park entrance and headquarters, situated in the heart of the park's amenities. It's a large campground with ample space for each campsite. The entire area is within a dense understory of spruce, cedars, and pines. Campsites are small but tucked into this understory; they provide privacy, quiet, and security to those who camp here. I sensed that these sites might be muddy during heavy rains.

Unlike most state parks, the campsites within the inner circle of all loops were laid out better than most. Interestingly, the first four sites were right inside the entrance, literally before you reach the main campground loop. These, as well as the other half a dozen sites on the right (southern) side of the campground road, were electrical and better suited for the bigger RVs.

Sites 4 through 23 make up the first loop. These are sites under a scattered canopy of aspen. Sites 7 and 8 have a denser understory than most. Site 11 is a good pick in this loop because it adjoins a rock escarpment and has plenty of space between it and its neighbors on either side. Sites 19 and 20 are long and narrow. This becomes really obvious when one looks up or down the driveways of either, as they are directly across from each other.

The sites in the second loop (24 through 37) and those in the third loop, 48 through 63, are more open, yet the area is thickly wooded with evergreens. Sites 59 through 62 are very open, offering little privacy.

My pick for a good site within these loops includes 72. It's an outside campsite at the end of the curve on the far loop. It's a long site that extends back into the woods. Just past its driveway is a path leading off to connect with the Civilian Conservation Corps Trail that runs east–west near the northern boundary of the park. This trail connects with several other trails

KEY INFORMATION

ADDRESS: 500 East MN 210 Carlton, MN 55718

OPERATED BY: Minnesota DNR, Division of Parks and Recreation

INFORMATION: (218) 384-4610

OPEN: Year-round

SITES: 80 semimodern sites, 21 electrical, 2 group sites, backpacking sites

ASSIGNMENT: First come, first served, unless reserved

REGISTRATION: At (866) 85-PARKS (72757), or online at www.stayatmn parks.com

FACILITIES: Water, restrooms, showers, playground, phone, water, trailer dump station

PARKING: On main campground road on left; at trailhead to the group sites

FEES: $7 daily permit, $5 group, $25 annual; camping fee $15 semimodern, $18 electric hookup $11 rustic; $8.50 nonrefundable reserve fee

ACTIVITIES: Waterfalls; extensive trail system, fishing, swinging bridge, whitewater rafting

RESTRICTIONS: Pets: On 6-foot maximum leash
Fires: In designated rings only
Alcohol: Not allowed
Vehicles: On designated trails or roads
Other: Closed to nonregistered guests 10 p.m.–8 a.m.

MAP

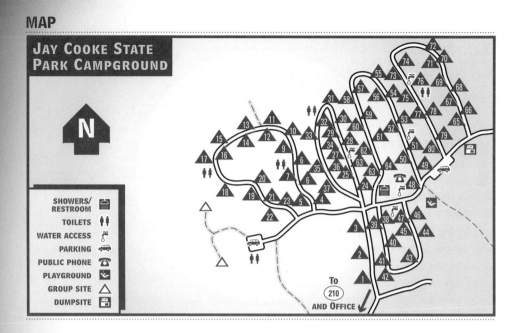

GETTING THERE

From Carlton, take MN 210 east 3 miles to the park entrance on the right. The park is also accessible from South Duluth by taking MN 23 about 9 miles south to MN 210. Go west about 6 miles to the park entrance on the left.

that combine to form a network stretching completely across the park's northern section.

In some areas, the dense screening between sites is due not to a thick understory but to the heavy lower branches of taller spruces and pines that fan out from the trunk and reach down to the ground.

LAKE ELMO PARK RESERVE CAMPGROUND

I'VE ALWAYS LIKED Lake Elmo Park Reserve. It's within minutes of downtown St. Paul and yet offers wide-open spaces, rolling hills, and clusters of woodlands scattered around several lakes. It also offers a variety of modern facilities and activities with ample opportunity to take long hikes through open spaces and pitch a tent in remote, "deep in the woods" campsites.

There are three types of campgrounds at Lake Elmo: modern, with the tight loops and close-proximity site configuration that too many campgrounds have these days; equestrian, which also serves as the overflow from the main campground that doesn't even have a name other than "modern;" and primitive, which is my favorite. Because you can park within about 150 yards of the farthest site, I decided that these five tent sites could qualify as drive-to sites. The few extra steps are worth it!

There are a few redeeming qualities about the modern site. The sites are open, inviting to the RV crowd, and have little shade. However, the shrubby vegetation, made up mostly of sumac, amur maple, and dogwood (mostly landscape accent plantings), provides a little privacy and gives a sense of personal space within the grounds' four loops.

If you must camp here, I suggest you try sites 55 through 60; these are at least backed by a wooded area. There are no tent sites across the road from this series, either, so you get a little more privacy. Beyond this string of acceptable sites sit sites 60 and 61, which are the beginning of the fourth campground loop. These two sites also back up to the stand of trees flanking this end of the modern campground. The remaining 70 sites are open, clustered, and typical. Definitely opt for those listed above or, better yet, push for the primitive area.

> *Five ample, easily accessible, and pleasantly primitive walk-in sites are set into the woods in a park offering many activities.*

RATINGS

Beauty: ☆ ☆ ☆
Privacy: ☆ ☆ ☆ ☆
Spaciousness: ☆ ☆ ☆
Quiet: ☆ ☆ ☆ ☆
Security: ☆ ☆ ☆
Cleanliness: ☆ ☆ ☆

ADDRESS: Washington County Parks
1515 Keats Avenue
Lake Elmo, MN
55042

OPERATED BY: Washington County Parks

INFORMATION: (651) 430-8368;
www.co.washington.
mn.us

OPEN: Year-round

SITES: 80 modern; 5 primitive (walk-in); 20 equestrian sites

ASSIGNMENT: First come, first served; unless reserved

REGISTRATION: At park office; $5 daily vehicle fee; reservations: (651) 430-8370, 2-night stay required for weekends

FACILITIES: Water

PARKING: At trailhead to walk-in sites

FEES: Walk-in sites: $4 non-refundable reservation fee; $15 sites with electricity

ACTIVITIES: Fishing, hiking, bird-watching at primitive sites; full park amenities nearby

RESTRICTIONS: **Pets:** Not allowed
Fires: In fire rings or grills only, cutting park trees and gathering firewood prohibited
Alcohol: Not allowed
Vehicles: No ATV use in the park
Other: 1 camp unit per site; 7-day stay limit; quiet hours 10 p.m.–7 a.m.

Five campsites, each one with its own earthy character, make up the string of sites in this section. Access to these sites is from a parking lot, along a 10-foot-wide grassy lane. This pathway winds to the right and then follows the edge of the woods as spurs to each campsite intersect it at short intervals.

Site 1 is off to the left and hidden by the edge of the forest that surrounds the small lake behind the first four sites. The campsite is modest: fire ring, picnic table, and tent space. Bur oak and ash are the main shade trees. A trail threads through the understory and heads down to the lake.

Sites 2 and 3 share the same access trail off the main grassy pathway. Site 2 has a small, earthen tent area, is flanked by shade trees, and has its own private walking path down to the lake. Site 3 is a short distance away—here your neighbor's volume level will dictate the peace and quiet this spot will afford. Site 3 is less shady than the other sites. Otherwise, it offers its own view of the lake through the underbrush as well as access to it via the earthen trail.

Site 4 is far from sites 2 and 3 and is situated on a flat area right above the lake's shore. This spot's earthen floor was covered with less grass than the other sites—this might be a bit muddy after a prolonged rain. Another concern is that this site lies only about five yards off the grass access trail. Heavy foot traffic will be more noticeable from site 4 than from any other site in the primitive area.

The last site, 5, is across from the access path to site 4. It sits back through a mature stand of aspens. It is also on a slope that rises from the lake and campsites 1 through 4 below, making it the only campsite in this group not near the small lake. Any of these sites would be a pleasant camping area for those who enjoy a more rustic experience. They sit halfway between Lake Elmo and Eagle Point Lake. (Eighty percent of Lake Elmo Park's 3.5 square miles of land is set aside for preservation and protection, and within that 80 percent lie two big lakes: Elmo and Eagle Point.)

Lake Elmo is a 206-acre lake with a depth of 130 feet and is the reserve's fishing hole. There are boat ramps and a fishing pier along its shore. A special

MAP

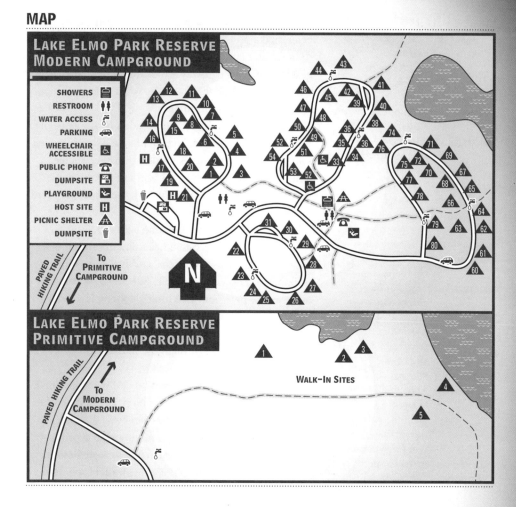

swimming pond has been created on land, just inland from the natural lake. This safe and clean swimming spot is a six-foot-deep, sandy-bottomed swimming area with a lifeguard.

Eagle Point Lake covers 143 acres. It is a good canoeing lake and also serves as a focal point for one of the park's longest hiking loops. A parking lot off the main park road puts hikers at one of several entry points on the lake's 3.7-mile loop.

The hike follows the lake's shoreline, taking one for a stroll through the meadows and along the forested areas of the western section of the reserve. This trail links with a half dozen other pathways that head even farther into the park's remote western and northwestern hill country. One loop follows the northern park boundary and connects with other trail networks at the equestrian campground.

GETTING THERE

From St. Paul head east on I-94; about 3 miles east of the intersection of I-694, turn left (north) at exit #251 on CR 19 and go about 1 mile to the park entrance.

MILLE LACS KATHIO STATE PARK CAMPGROUND

> *This camp is rich in Native American heritage and nestled in a hardwood forest amid rolling glacial terrain.*

THIS AREA IS TYPICAL of the lakes region of Minnesota, in which glaciers played a major role. Besides the 18-mile-wide Mille Lacs Lake that is the remnants of a much larger lake, the evidence of that ice age history is in the hills formed by the glacial moraine of those receding rivers of ice. Take those hills and cover them with second-generation growth of maples, oaks, and other hardwoods and you have Mille Lacs Kathio State Park. Add a few spruce tree clusters here and there, and you've enhanced this park into one of the prettier ones in the state. The fall colors alone are a reason to visit here.

The Mille Lacs area is rich in Native American history, from ancient tribes from the Old Copper Tradition dating back over 4,000 years, to the early Dakota people, a band called the Mdewakanton—"the people who live by the water of the Great Spirit." More recently, the area has been inhabited by Ojibwe, a band of northern woodland Indians who drove the Dakota farther west onto the plains.

Today the popularity of Mille Lacs Kathio is tied to the popular lake, famous for its walleye fishing. It's also the origin of the Rum River—a river much used for recreation by the time it reaches the cities just north of Minneapolis. The Rum River flows out of Ogechie Lake, itself a small lake formed by a stream flowing out of Mille Lacs. Fishing and boating are two very popular pastimes at this park.

Ogechie Campground is closest to the lake that bears the same name. Campsites 1 through 26 are in the higher elevations of the park. The sites are moderately small but are staggered throughout the campground to offer a bit of privacy from campers across the road. A solid alder and birch understory provides additional screening between each site. It's a better layout than most Minnesota state park campgrounds. The

RATINGS

Beauty: ✿ ✿ ✿ ✿
Privacy: ✿ ✿ ✿
Spaciousness: ✿ ✿ ✿
Quiet: ✿ ✿ ✿
Security: ✿ ✿ ✿
Cleanliness: ✿ ✿ ✿ ✿

variety of tall oaks and maples makes the area seem more northern in setting than it really is (it's only about 80 miles from the Twin Cities).

The Petaga Campground is a multiuse cluster of campsites, walk-ins, and cabins. Sites 27 through 63 are long and staggered—and the first choice of the RV crowd. There is ample vegetation between the sites, and the bur oak overstory makes the long, narrow sites somewhat private. However, turn-outs and the long pull-ins all indicate that this is where the big-wheeled units need to camp.

Just across the park road from the lower site are the walk-ins, five cabins, and what must be considered the overflow campground. The walk-ins and the overflow are the most private and most secluded camping areas in the park!

The three walk-in sites, 64 through 66, are up a ridge only 30 to 50 yards from the parking lot at the end of the cabin road cul-de-sac. Although they share the same knoll, they are spaced well apart. A water source, parking, and a toilet are right at the base of the trail leading to the three sites.

Literally stuck behind the cabins are four more tent sites. These spin off from the cul-de-sac spur leading from the main park road. Each site is well apart from the others and within an easy walk of a main trail spur. With water and a toilet at the start of the camping circle, it seemed to me the best place to camp—even if it was in the distant backyard of the cabins. It looks out of place on the map, and even as you drive in, but it works!

Hiking is a big activity in this park. In the northern section, trails are networked around and over countless hills and valleys carved from the ancient terminal moraine. One can hike to the observation tower (on shared horse trails—be careful) or to several sites along the shore of Ogechie Lake. Trails cut close to each of the two main campgrounds. An elongated loop of horse trails cuts through the center of the park; hikers can also use this trail, although hiking is probably more enjoyable where horses aren't allowed.

A leisurely paddle by canoe or kayak is possible by putting in at a boat ramp at the end of the road that goes past the group camp. You can then paddle

KEY INFORMATION

ADDRESS:	15066 Kathio State Park Road Onamia, MN 56359
OPERATED BY:	Minnesota DNR, Division of Parks and Recreation
INFORMATION:	(320) 532-3523
OPEN:	Year-round
SITES:	20 electrical, 2 wheelchair accessible, 19 semimodern (3 walk-in), 26 rustic; 1 group site
ASSIGNMENT:	First come, first served, unless reserved
REGISTRATION:	At (866) 85-PARKS (72757) or online at www.stayatmn parks.com
FACILITIES:	Restroom, showers, water, dumpster
PARKING:	At entrance to walk-in sites; first loop of Petaga Campground
FEES:	$7 daily permit, $5 group, $25 annual; camping fee $15 semimodern, $18 electric hookup; $11 rustic; $8.50 nonrefundable reserve fee
ACTIVITIES:	Picnic, playground, swimming beach, interpretive center, canoe and rowboat rental, hiking trails, riding trails
RESTRICTIONS:	Pets: On 6-foot maximum leash Fires: In designated rings only Alcohol: Not allowed Vehicles: On designated trails or roads Other: Closed to nonregistered campers 10 p.m.– 8 a.m.

MAP

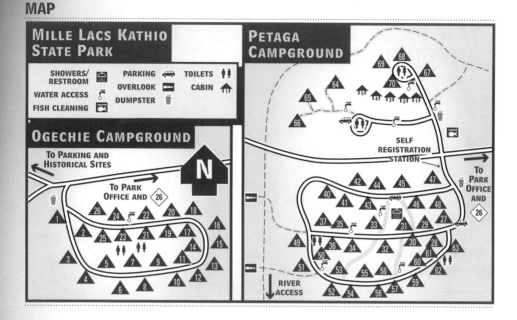

MILLE LACS KATHIO STATE PARK

- SHOWERS/RESTROOM
- WATER ACCESS
- FISH CLEANING
- PARKING
- OVERLOOK
- DUMPSTER
- TOILETS
- CABIN

OGECHIE CAMPGROUND

To Parking and Historical Sites

To Park Office and 26

N

PETAGA CAMPGROUND

SELF REGISTRATION STATION

To Park Office and 26

RIVER ACCESS

GETTING THERE

From Onamia, go 7 miles north on US 169 to CR 26. Turn left (west) on CR 26 and go 1 mile to the park entrance on the right.

upstream into Ogechie Lake or take the current downriver to Shakopee Lake where a boat landing on the southern shore is right on CR 26 (it's about 2.5 miles back to the park entrance).

Wildlife viewers will have many opportunities to witness hawks, osprey, owls, and eagles in action. A bird list is available at the park office. Deer, beavers, and raccoons are also common within the park.

There is also a Native American museum outside the park and just a few miles north on US 169 that showcases the proud heritage of the people of this area.

Whether it's cultural or geological history or the richly colored and lush hardwood forest setting, Mille Lacs Kathio offers a better-than-average camping experience for those who decide to pitch their tent here.

ST. CROIX STATE PARK CAMPGROUNDS

YOU WOULD THINK that the state's largest park—with over 33,000 acres—would have better campsites! They are really packed in among the three loops that form the collective campground at St. Croix State Park. Still, there are a few good areas among these tightly spaced loops to select a couple of good places to pitch your tent.

The setting, laid out in the V formed by the Kettle River flowing into the St. Croix River, is one of great forests and extensive ridges along crystal-clear rivers. Over 21 miles of the St. Croix forms the eastern boundary of the park and at least ten other streams course their way through the area. Vast forests of white and red pine once protected this huge drainage area. The late 1800s saw the emergence of timber harvesting. These hills are now a mix of post–timber harvested spruce, sugar maples, and oak hardwoods and even tamarack swamps.

In the 1930s much of this logged area was sold for farmland. Those farms didn't do so well, and programs were found to convert large amounts of acreage to recreation. St. Croix State Park began as a recreation demonstration area and was established as a state park in 1943.

All the available electric hookups are located in the Riverview Campground loop. Better sites are found in the second (Paint Rock Springs) and third (Old Logging Trail) loops. All sites are laid out in the typical state park formula—an access driveway forming relatively tight, elongated loops. Each site has a picnic table, fire ring, and space for at least one tent.

Paint Rock Springs Campground has over 60 sites alone. Site 64 is large, especially for a park that has so many small sites. The forest understory is made up mostly of paper birch and young red and jack pine trees. Sites 70 through 80 are close together, open

> *You'll find two of the upper Midwest's most notable wild and scenic rivers, the St. Croix and the Kettle, here.*

RATINGS

Beauty: ✿ ✿
Privacy: ✿ ✿
Spaciousness: ✿ ✿
Quiet: ✿ ✿
Security: ✿ ✿ ✿
Cleanliness: ✿ ✿ ✿ ✿

ADDRESS: 30065 St. Croix Park Road
Hinckley, MN 55037

OPERATED BY: Minnesota DNR, Division of Parks and Recreation

INFORMATION: (320) 384-6591; (651) 296-6157 (from metro area); (888) 646-6367

OPEN: Year-round

SITES: 215 campsites (42 electrical), 1 primitive group; 6 backpack and 11 canoe sites

ASSIGNMENT: First come, first served, unless reserved

REGISTRATION: At (866) 85-PARKS (72757), or online at www.stayatmn parks.com

FACILITIES: Electricity, water, restroom, showers, store, bicycle/canoe rental, phone, lodge

PARKING: Across from picnic area; near each campground

FEES: $7 daily permit, $5 group, $25 annual; camping $15 semi-modern, $18 electric, $11 rustic, $7.50 wheelchair-accessible; $8.50 nonrefundable reserve fee

ACTIVITIES: Bike trails, canoeing, hiking trails

RESTRICTIONS: Pets: On 6-foot maximum leash
Fires: In designated rings only
Alcohol: Not allowed
Vehicles: On designated trails or roads
Other: Closed to nonregistered guests 10 p.m.–8 a.m.

spacing—"communal" camping. As with most loop configurations, however, those outside the roadway are my pick—particularly site 91 because it's not only on the outer loop but also at the head of the loop and backs onto the undeveloped forested area.

Sites 106 through 120 reminded me of a big playground with campsites shoulder to shoulder along the inner loop. However, sites 112 and 114, though open, were much more spacious. Sites 121 and 122 were in the woods and had little understory privacy screening but were farther apart than most.

The third loop, Old Logging Trail Campground, offers more of the same although site 141 stood out as excellent—lots of privacy among stands of jack pine. Sites in the second loop in this section are backed by a stand of young spruce trees. By the time the loop reaches site 170, there is more understory and better spacing between the sites. This is especially true for sites 190 through 199.

The last loop included my favorite site in this park, 211. It sits way back in the woods, and even though the driveways here tend to be opposite each site, the sites on the outside of the loop are set back far enough to make up the privacy in distance from the road. Another good site in this loop is 215. The section of higher-numbered sites is arguably the best section of the park in which to camp.

All these loops are off the main park road, which parallels the St. Croix River. The entire course of the river is traced by trails accessible from every loop in the park. Trails abound throughout the park to keep hikers happy (be advised that most hiking trails are shared by horseback riders, too). You can hike along the entire length of the Kettle River course through the park. There are many overlooks, especially in the western half of the park, accessible by those trails. You can also drive right up to the base of the observation tower for grand views down toward the Kettle River.

This is a glaciated region, and the St. Croix valley has an exceptional variety of soil types. Most of these can be seen along the River Bluff Trail. Some of these soils are composed of clay, notably a yellow variety that

MAP

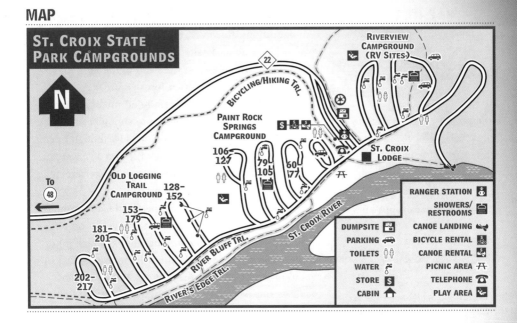

St. Croix State Park Campgrounds

is heavily deposited along points on the trail. Check the park map for sections of the trail called yellow banks.

And, because it's the St. Croix, expect to see a lot of canoe traffic along the river. There are several put-in points within the park to allow you to arrange short shuttles for quick trips downriver without ever leaving the park.

GETTING THERE

From the Twin Cities, take I-35 north and take the exit for Hinckley. Go east 15 miles on MN 48 to the park entrance at the intersection with CR 22. Turn right into the park entrance.

SIBLEY
STATE PARK
CAMPGROUND

Serpentine, tree-covered ridges and hills in an old forest setting characterize Sibley.

SEEMS LIKE EVERY state park in southern Minnesota is located at the heart or edge of a key natural history area. This is no truer than at Sibley State Park, situated in that area of Minnesota where the eastern edge of the expansive great prairies meets the hardwood forests of the Big Woods region beyond those grasses. It's an area where an even more ancient history reveals a landscape strewn with the rock and rubble debris from four glaciated periods in this region's prehistory.

The lake and hills of Sibley Park are recurring geological reminders of the receding ice fields and melting monolithic chunks of glaciers that left their marks on this region of not only Minnesota but the entire upper Midwest. The shoreline of the lake drops away sharply to the bottom—no long sloping shelf to a shallow depth. These are glacier-born lakes—characteristic bodies of water formed when huge chunks of glacial ice, once embedded in the landscape, melted away, filling those gaping holes with water. Those lakes are surrounded by ridges and hills formed when gigantic drain fields from retreating ice melts spewed gravel and boulders out across the plains, sometimes through melted channels in the ice, to form long fingers of ridges and large piles of gravel-turned-hills. Today, those harsh reminders are subdued by tree-lined hills, ridges, and knolls and flowing prairie grasses with clusters of renegade sumacs and the occasional gnarly oak sapling.

That topography in miniature describes Oak Ridge, the upper campground at Sibley. The site is forested with mature oaks, maple, and ash—all classic Big Tree species. This defined overstory has an equally mature and dense understory. The first irregularly shaped loop containing campsites 75 through 98 straddles a line of open savannah-like grasses and an oak scrub that quickly develops into a thick canopy within

RATINGS

Beauty: ✿ ✿ ✿
Privacy: ✿ ✿ ✿
Spaciousness: ✿ ✿ ✿
Quiet: ✿ ✿ ✿
Security: ✿ ✿ ✿
Cleanliness:✿ ✿ ✿ ✿

a few campsites of the entrance to this loop. Each site is tucked back into the surrounding vegetation with the standard utilities of fire ring and picnic table.

The staggered entrance driveway to each site along a narrow, serpentine road creates secluded and private camping sites throughout the first loop. As the road winds back out from the campgrounds, the last few sites, 92 through 95, become more open again.

The second loop contains sites 99 through 131, which are all laid out in an open array with little understory. The middle section of this equally hilly campground with the serpentine road through it does get more wooded as one approaches sites 106 through 121.

Toilet stations and a restroom and shower unit, along with the six water pumps scattered throughout the two sites, give all campers easy access.

The lower campground, Lakeview, offers extra-spacious sites on the standard grid-like layout seen at many state parks. Box elders and maples dominate the forested area that is otherwise so open it resembles a picnic area—and RV park. That said, campsites 66 through 68, and 70, at least merge into the uncluttered woods behind each of those sites, offering a bit of the better life of tent camping.

No matter which loop or site you choose, take some time to check out the hiking trails—all 18 miles' worth. Make sure you include the trail that leads up to the all-encompassing vantage point at the top of Mount Tom. There you'll enjoy a colorful panoramic vista of the forests and countryside. The passage along the paved trail that winds through a quaint stand of oaks as it climbs to the summit soon reveals the 360-degree view. Your imagination may help you create a prehistoric landscape of when mile-high ice fields covered this area. A trip to the summit of Mount Tom at the height of fall color would be one well worth planning.

Pay close attention when hiking the network of trails; they may reveal some of the park's critters—whitetail deer, ruffed grouse, fox, and more. The marsh areas are great for wildlife viewing. Be on the watch for puddle ducks, egrets, and a variety of songbirds.

KEY INFORMATION

ADDRESS: 800 Sibley Park Road NE New London, MN 56273-9664

OPERATED BY: Minnesota DNR, Division of Parks and Recreation

INFORMATION: (320) 354-2005

OPEN: Year-round

SITES: 134 semimodern/ 3 50-capacity group sites

ASSIGNMENT: First come, first served, unless reserved

REGISTRATION: At (866) 85-PARKS (72757), or reserve online at www.stay atmnparks.com

FACILITIES: Restrooms, showers, water, trailer dump station

PARKING: On right just before entering Lakeview Campground

FEES: $7 daily permit, $5 group, $25 annual; camping $15 semimodern, $18 electric hookup, $11 rustic; $8.50 nonrefundable reservation fee

ACTIVITIES: Horseback riding trails, bike and hiking trails, swimming, fishing pier, boat ramp, overlooks

RESTRICTIONS: Pets: On 6-foot maximum leash Fires: In designated rings only Alcohol: Not allowed Vehicles: On designated trails or roads Other: Closed to nonregistered campers 10 p.m.–8 a.m.

MAP

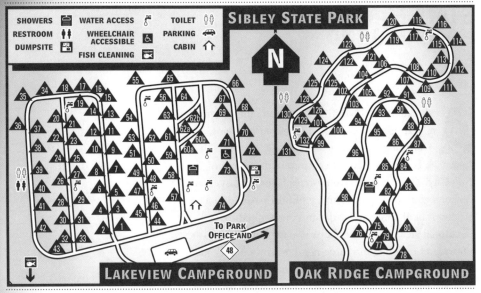

GETTING THERE

Go 15 miles north of Wilmar on US 71 to CR 48. Take a left onto CR 48 and go about 1 mile to the park entrance.

The rumpled hills, winding roads, and mature stands all create a deep-woods setting, laced with hiking trails and dotted with lakes—a camper's delight.

SNAKE RIVER STATE FOREST CAMPGROUND

ANY CAMPGROUND TUCKED among the towering mixed pines along a medium-sized canoeing river is a good choice in my book. So it is with the Snake River State Forest campground just east of Pine City. This is within Minnesota's Chengwatana State Forest, a glacier-sculpted country of hills covered in a modest mix of white and red pines interrupted by an occasional jack pine and clumps of paper birch. It's also a terrain of marshes and three notable rivers: the Kettle, Snake, and St. Croix. Although the Snake doesn't carry the lofty wild and scenic river status of its companions, it's a fun river to paddle.

For hikers, the Snake River campground offers a place to rest, as well as access to the state's Munger Trail. This multiple-use trail cuts across the road leading to the campground—right inside the entrance after you turning off County Road 8.

You know you are getting closer to the north country when you see notices about black bears on the information bulletin board. The warning is not exclusive to the Snake River sites and should be heeded as a general practice. Common sense should prevail when preparing or storing food.

Campsites are laid out along two loops under a canopy of white and red pines and other mixed near-north species. These sites are usually sitting back off the roadway and have ample understory for privacy and security. Each site is laid out with the standard-issue picnic table and fire ring. There are no designated pads for a tent, just plenty of grassy spaces to pitch it.

Sites 1 through 5 are spaced far apart on either side of the first loop, under a canopy of red pines. Site 5 sits up from the river by itself with only the picnic area nearby. There is a stairway made of timbers leading down toward the river just beyond campsite 5.

> *Bring your canoe to this charming setting with the Snake River as a backdrop.*

RATINGS

Beauty: ✿ ✿ ✿
Privacy: ✿ ✿ ✿
Spaciousness: ✿ ✿ ✿
Quiet: ✿ ✿ ✿ ✿
Security: ✿ ✿ ✿
Cleanliness: ✿ ✿ ✿ ✿

ADDRESS: c/o Wild River State Park
39797 Park Trail
Center City, MN 55012

OPERATED BY: Managed by Wild River State Park (see also: Minnesota DNR, Division of Forestry, (651) 296-6157)

INFORMATION: (651) 583-2125

OPEN: Year-round

SITES: 26 rustic sites

ASSIGNMENT: First come, first served

REGISTRATION: Not available

FACILITIES: Vault toilets, water

PARKING: On left before entrance to campground loops

FEES: $10 per night

ACTIVITIES: Canoeing, fishing

RESTRICTIONS: Pets: Must be kept on leash
Fires: Must be in cleared areas at least 5 feet around and built less than 3 feet in diameter
Alcohol: Not allowed
Vehicles: No motorized vehicles on any nonmotorized trails or in posted areas that prohibit use
Other: Hunting and firearms only in posted areas; camping possible in undeveloped areas (special rules apply)

There is only one picnic table in this area, but it's a great place to get close to the river without going through a campsite.

Site 6 backs onto another site (16) in the next loop but is really the only campsite so situated—yet even it is spacious. The rest of the sites in this first loop are spread out, staggered off the main loop, and spacious. Site 11 is close to the main road, making it the least desirable site in this loop.

The second loop offers more sites backing up to the river. Site 12 is more open than most of the sites in this campground, but like the rest it is in a staggered layout, so there's privacy and room to play at this site as well. Sites 14 and 15 are in a cluster of white and red pine. Sites 16 (close to 6 in the first loop) and 17 are nondescript sites, but they are private and spacious.

Sites 18 and 19 are at the head of the loop and up from the big 90-degree bend that the Snake River takes at this point in the campground. These sites located up from the river usually have a well-worn path leading from the campsite to the bank. In fact, there is a defined trail between sites 18 and 19 that leads down to the river from the loop. It connects to an informal but defined trail that heads up- and downstream from that point.

Sites 20 and 22 are in the open, site 20 a little too close to the outhouse for my liking. Sites 23 through 25 are in a stand of pines and aspen and sit on a plateau about 15 feet above the river. The river is a smooth-flowing body of water at this point, so there are no riffles or rock gardens to create any noticeable river sounds. Still, its proximity to the center of the campsite makes these sites especially appealing. Site 26 is right off the road, and is the smallest of the sites in the campground.

Every site at the Snake River Campground offers pleasant surroundings. The canopy of mixed pines, the spaciousness of the sites, and the river defining the boundaries on two sides all combine to create a pleasant and casual camping environment. Canoeing campers may want to consider a shuttle to enable them to either put in or take out at this campground during a weekend paddling outing.

MAP

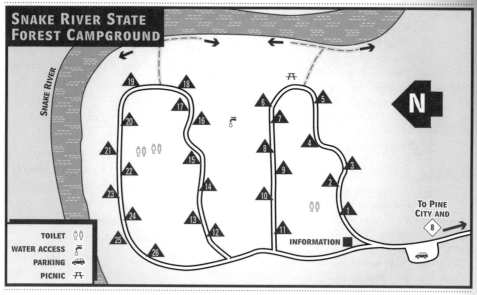

SNAKE RIVER STATE FOREST CAMPGROUND

SNAKE RIVER

TOILET	🚻
WATER ACCESS	🚰
PARKING	🚗
PICNIC	🏕

INFORMATION

To Pine City and

8

GETTING THERE

From Pine City, take CR 8 east 9 miles to the park entrance on the left.

WILD RIVER STATE PARK CAMPGROUND

> *This beautifully forested park stretches several miles along the scenic and alluring St. Croix River.*

ANY TIME YOU GET A CHANCE to enjoy camping along the St. Croix, do it. The farther north you can get, away from the larger communities closer to the Twin Cities, the purer the experience will be. Wild River State Park offers campers spacious sites, wonderful hiking trails, river access with a few shoreside campsites, and dense Minnesota hardwood forests. The park is long and narrow, stretching for a dozen or so miles right along the west bank of the wild and scenic St. Croix River.

Although there are several good sites within the developed campground, I've only pitched my tent at one of the walk-in sites along the river. A few are close enough that you can park nearby and make short trips to the campsite. Others are a bit farther apart and are actually better accessed by the river. These are rustic sites by definition but offer a basic tent space, picnic table, fire ring, and pit toilet. The sites are in isolated spots along the river and are accessible by canoe or by the trail that follows along the riverbank. If you are a self-sufficient camper who wants to be away from even the smallest gathering of tents, these sites are for you. However, if you are bound to the land or don't want the long haul, check out the five loops at the northern end of the southern section of this park.

Oak, ash, maple, and aspen form a dense, lush forest with a solid understory in which five loops of the campground are situated. Immediately on entering Loop A, you notice the spaciousness of each site. The sites are spread out, the driveways are staggered in most cases, and each site is surrounded by a thick understory providing a lot of privacy. As is the nature of a looped campground, those sites situated along the outside of the loop offer more room and less likelihood of neighbors pitching a tent too close.

Loops B and C are more open than Loop A, but

RATINGS

Beauty: ✿ ✿ ✿
Privacy: ✿ ✿ ✿ ✿
Spaciousness: ✿ ✿ ✿ ✿
Quiet: ✿ ✿ ✿ ✿ ✿
Security: ✿ ✿ ✿
Cleanliness: ✿ ✿ ✿ ✿

each loop is separated from the other to provide some room to spread out. A little creative tent pitching through these sites will ensure a seemingly private experience in the woods with few line-of-sight views of the tent next door or across the road.

A thick canopy of bur and red oak protects the sites in Loop D. This is coupled with a thick understory that continues throughout Loop E. As with the earlier loops, these sites are equally spacious and offer considerable privacy. At the head of each loop is a trail that directs campers to the St. Croix River flowing down the densely wooded bank just beyond the campsite.

It's no surprise that the campsites are spacious—this is one of the largest parks in the state. Nearly 5,000 of its 6,800-plus acres were donated as park property by Northern States Power Company. Its human history traces back past the white pine timber days, before early fur-trading routes, beyond even the Dakota and Ojibwe tribes to nomadic inhabitants who first settled this area over 6,000 years ago.

The most impressive amenities of this park, besides the river and woods, are the 15 miles of hiking trails. Trails vary from the wide berth of the old military roadway running up through the center of the park to the narrow, earthen path along the river. There's even 2.5 miles of handicapped-accessible trail. A horseback riding stable is located right outside the park to accommodate the cowpoke spirit in campers. The park provides over 20 miles of horse trails, too!

Not all of this park is wooded. The Amador Prairie is a small bluestem prairie system that seems to flow throughout the park between the islands of trees like a great sea of grass. Because of these two distinct ecosystems, and the proximity of the river and patches of marsh areas in the park, wildlife abounds. Whitetail deer find the forest/grass mix a perfect habitat, while the waterways are home or stopover spots for a variety of ducks, herons, and bitterns. Raptors such as harriers and bald eagles hunt the valleys and prairies for prey.

For wide, roomy, deep-forest camping or a weekend jaunt in the canoe with the chance at a secluded

KEY INFORMATION

ADDRESS: 39797 Park Trail Center City, MN 55012

OPERATED BY: Minnesota DNR, Division of Parks and Recreation

INFORMATION: (651) 583-2125

OPEN: Year-round

SITES: 96 semimodern, 8 canoe, 8 backpack

ASSIGNMENT: First come, first served, unless reserved

REGISTRATION: At (866) 85-PARKS (72757), or online at www.stayatmn parks.com

FACILITIES: Restrooms, showers, water, trailer sanitation station, boat ramp, shelter, visitor center, amphitheater

PARKING: At head of loop D, at all boat ramps, and at picnic area before campground

FEES: $7 daily permit, $5 group, $25 annual; camping $15 semimodern, $18 electric hookup, $15 rustic, $7 backpack; $8.50 nonrefundable reservation fee

ACTIVITIES: Horseback riding trails, bike and hiking trails, boat ramp, canoeing

RESTRICTIONS: Pets: On 6-foot maximum leash
Fires: In rings only
Alcohol: Not allowed
Vehicles: On designated trails or roads
Other: Closed to nonregistered campers 10 p.m.–8 a.m.

MAP

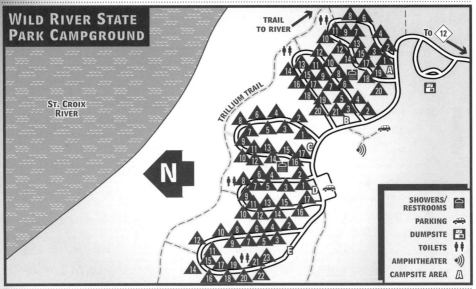

GETTING THERE

Take I-35 from the Twin Cities, exit at MN 95 (Exit 147 at Cambridge). Take MN 95 northeast 14 miles to Almelund. Go north on CR 12 about 3 miles to the park's main (southern) entrance.

site along a wild and scenic river, camping at Wild River State Park ranks up there with the best of the best in my book.

WILLIAM O'BRIEN STATE PARK CAMPGROUND

Marine on St. Croix

I **USED TO CANOE DOWN** the St. Croix River to William O'Brien Park from Taylor's Falls when I was in college. During all those stopovers I never once realized that there was another whole section of the park across the highway from the river. It wasn't until I explored the hiking trails in this upper section that I learned of its character and charm. Fortunately for campers seeking the more peaceful and private camping experience, both sections of the park have a few sites that make the list here.

Each unit of the park has its own campground with about 60 sites each. At first glance the campgrounds are characteristically "state park" in appearance. They have the standard-issue picnic table, fire ring, and drive-in parking space. The upper campground is made up of four loops, each to the left off the main road. This road skirts a marshy area on the west (right side of the road). It's not until you get to the third and fourth loops, campsites 97 through 124, that sites are laid out along both sides. This opens up possibilities—camping on the outside of the loops is usually the best option because the back of one lane of campsites doesn't back up to those in the next lane. The last loop is a cul-de-sac and offers about a dozen campsites, and although they are fairly open, not so private, and close to the road, they are still the preferred picks in this section.

The trails in the western half of the park (this upper section) wind through hills and meadows, around small lakes, and even across or under railroad tracks, creating a meandering country footpath network that can keep hikers trekking merrily along for miles.

The lower campground is a tight cluster of sites laid out in a single loop, and a loop intersected by a narrow road down the center of the campground creating a double loop. The odd numbered sites from 1 to

> *This is almost like two different parks—the upper park with its forests, meadows, and hills, and the lower park with the forested, scenic St. Croix River.*

RATINGS

Beauty: ✩ ✩ ✩
Privacy: ✩ ✩ ✩
Spaciousness: ✩ ✩ ✩
Quiet: ✩ ✩ ✩
Security: ✩ ✩ ✩
Cleanliness: ✩ ✩ ✩

ADDRESS: 16821 O'Brien Trail
North
Marine on St. Croix,
MN 55047

OPERATED BY: Minnesota DNR,
Division of Parks
and Recreation

INFORMATION: (651) 433-0500

OPEN: Year-round

SITES: 125 semimodern;
50-capacity group;
90-capacity pioneer
group camp

ASSIGNMENT: First come, first
served, unless
reserved

REGISTRATION: At (866) 85-PARKS
(72757), or online at
www.stayatmn
parks.com

FACILITIES: Restrooms, showers,
vault toilets, water

PARKING: In lower and upper
campgrounds

FEES: $7 daily permit, $5
group, $25 annual;
camping $15 semi-
modern, $18 electric
hookup, $11 rustic;
$8.50 nonrefundable
reservation fee

ACTIVITIES: Swimming, canoeing, boating, fishing,
hiking trails, access
to county bike trail,
interpretive center

RESTRICTIONS: Pets: Must be on a
leash no longer than
6 feet
Fires: In designated
rings only
Alcohol: Not allowed
Vehicles: On desig-
nated trails or roads
Other: Closed to
nonregistered
campers 10 p.m.–
8 a.m.

11 are those outside loop locations that back up to low-land trees and understory.

At the opposite end of the looped campground, sites 47 through 53 on the outside of the loop are the preferred spots if you don't like neighbors on both sides of your tent. These sites are also more spread out, a feature none of the inner circle can claim.

The area's topography is glacial valleys and hills created from the sandstone deposited by an inland sea several millennia ago. The first settlers were the Dakota and Ojibwe. Later, a booming fur trade flourished, followed by a prosperous timber industry. Numerous sawmills rose up along the St. Croix until the white pines were depleted. Today the area is a rich center of tourism with Taylor's Falls to the north and the bustling river town of Stillwater to the south.

Of course, William O'Brien State Park is considered a canoer's park because of its location on the St. Croix River. Besides the attraction of paddling the river's main channel and back sloughs above and below the park, William O' Brien tends to be as popular as the take-out spot for casual river runners starting up at Interstate Park or for those putting in at the park and paddling south a dozen or so miles to Stillwater. Either way, the canoeing in this region is hot all summer long. Shuttle services and canoe rentals near the park provide helpful services, too.

To be honest, I wasn't sure William O' Brien State Park should be on this list. The campgrounds are typical. This is a wonderful park, so close to the Twin Cities, and offers myriad opportunities to enjoy nature, both physically and mentally. The lower camping area has the personality of a park on water's edge, and the upper park reveals the personality of its varied terrain and mixture of woods and meadows, flats, and rolling hills. It's a dual-personality park to be enjoyed fully on both fronts.

Whether you're in need of a weekend getaway or are passing through, spending some time in both halves of William O' Brien State Park will offer rewards the entire family can enjoy.

MAP

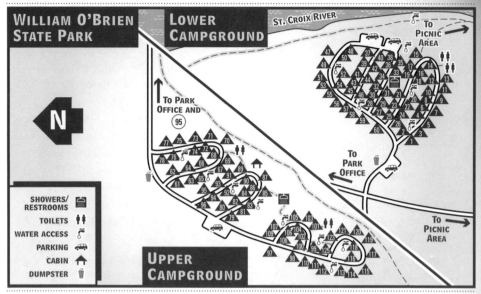

From Stillwater, take MN 95 north 13 miles to the park's entrance.

SOUTHERN MINNESOTA

BEAVER CREEK VALLEY STATE PARK CAMPGROUNDS

THIS QUAINT, NARROW creek valley showcases the diverse flora, fauna, and geological offerings of the extreme southeastern portion of Minnesota. It offers a unique contradiction to the glacier-worn terrain common to most Midwestern states around the Great Lakes region.

Beaver Creek Valley lies in what's called the Driftless area of glaciation. It was not covered by the last great Ice Age about 10,000 years ago. Still, its makeup was directly affected by surrounding ice—massive sheets that retreated, spewing torrents of water that formed valley-gouging rivers throughout this area. Etching its way through layers of sandstone and dolomite, these unrelenting rivers carved out myriad valleys—such as those that form Beaver Creek Valley. Subsequent forestation by lowland willows, cottonwoods, and elm, and groves of maples and oaks higher up the slopes have turned this area into a modern living museum of rare plants, abundant wildlife, and beautiful valleys laced with spring-fed creeks. Evidence of activity by Native Americans and homesteading settlers who relied on the park's resources can be found here as well.

The most striking impressions of the park are visual. On entering the park campers will immediately notice the steep-walled valleys. Long but narrow and winding roads (not really conducive to battleship-sized RVs) lead campers through groves of bottomland trees and into upland hardwoods to three camping areas. The road twists through the modern day-use and picnic area before reaching the first, large campsite stretched out along the roadway. Its sites are more open and spacious and offer the least amount of privacy of the three sites in the park. Be advised that early spring flooding could spread to this campground (particularly sites 1 through 14) during spring thaw and

> *This nature lover's gem is nestled in the valleys of Southeast Minnesota's beautiful 'Driftless' area.*

RATINGS

Beauty: ☆ ☆ ☆
Privacy: ☆ ☆
Spaciousness: ☆ ☆
Quiet: ☆ ☆ ☆
Security: ☆ ☆ ☆
Cleanliness: ☆ ☆ ☆ ☆

ADDRESS: 15954 County Road 1
Caledonia, MN
55921-8653

OPERATED BY: Minnesota DNR,
Division of Parks
and Recreation

INFORMATION: (507) 724-2107

OPEN: All year

SITES: 26 semi-modern, 16
rustic, 6 walk-in

ASSIGNMENT: First come, first
served, unless
reserved

REGISTRATION: Available by calling
(866) 85-PARKS
(72757), or reserve
online at www.stay
atmnparks.com

FACILITIES: Restrooms, showers,
vault toilets, water

PARKING: At campsites, visitor
center and north
entrance to Beaver
Creek Valley Trail

FEES: $7 daily permit; $5
group, $25 annual;
camping fee $15
semimodern, $18
electric hookup, $11
rustic; $8.50 nonre-
fundable reservation
fee

ACTIVITIES: Stream fishing for
trout; 8 miles of
hiking trails

RESTRICTIONS: Pets: Must be on a
leash no longer than
6 feet
Fires: In designated
fire rings only
Alcohol: Not allowed
Vehicles: On
designated trails or
roads only
Other: Closed to
nonregistered
campers 10 p.m.–
8 a.m.

high overflow. These are the sites most likely to be used by the RV crowd.

The designated tent campground is a quarter mile beyond this and is nestled into the valley just beyond Big Spring, the official source of East Beaver Creek. Typical of all state parks, the site includes a pull-in driveway, picnic table, and fire ring. A pit toilet as well as restrooms and shower units are within easy walking distance.

My choice for camping here is any one of the six walk-in/group sites. Though the park offers many amenities and any site is adequate and worthwhile, the walk-in sites offer that feeling of remoteness and rustic-ity that reminds me of what camping has always been about—a chance to experience the outdoors, a reprieve from the madding crowd. These sites are off a cul-de-sac about a half mile past the tent campground. As in most state parks, the few extra yards of carrying gear to your walk-in site are rewarded with privacy, soli-tude, and a sense of truly being away from it all.

If you're the inquisitive type and love nature, Beaver Creek Valley will keep you entertained and informed on many short visits or a long, active week-end. Trails follow the main flowages and take hikers up to the ridges and plateaus 250 feet above the valley floor. Beaver Valley Trail is a 5-mile out-and-back trek along the valley floor. Plateau Rock Trail rises to a ridge-top plateau on one side of the valley, and the Switchback Trail zigzags up the other side—both reward hikers with panoramic overlooks across the valley and beyond.

One of the things I remember about this camping area is that warnings are posted around the park about the timber rattlesnake common to this part of Min-nesota but very elusive. Caution should be taken when hiking or climbing remote trails. More likely you'll encounter the deer, fox, raccoon, and occasional turkey who live in the park.

Beaver Creek Valley affords anglers young and old an opportunity to wet a line—the creeks are team-ing with native (not stocked!) brown trout.

Catching an elusive brownie, hiking along and up steep valley trails, scouting for wildlife, or just enjoying

MAP

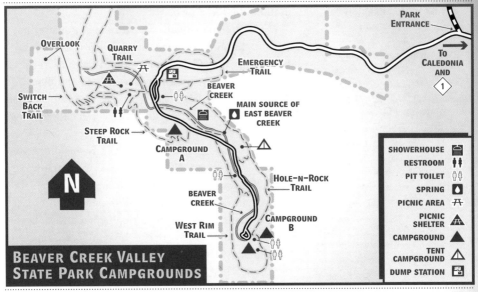

BEAVER CREEK VALLEY
STATE PARK CAMPGROUNDS

the plethora of wildflowers that bloom throughout the summer makes Beaver Creek Valley a top choice among these already special places to camp in Minnesota.

GETTING THERE

Coming south on either MN 76 or MN 44 toward Caledonia, turn right (west) onto CR 1 and continue 5 miles to the park entrance.

BLUE MOUNDS STATE PARK CAMPGROUND

> *Campers share the prairie with Minnesota cactus, coyotes, and a wild herd of buffalo at Blue Mounds.*

To geologists, Blue Mounds are outcroppings of Sioux quartzite that juts out across a mile-and-a-half of western Minnesota prairie (Blue Mounds is one of the largest expanses of prairie found in the state's park system). To pioneers crossing this prairie, these bumps on the western skyline appeared blue—hence the name. Since the first three American bison were introduced here in 1961, Blue Mounds has become home to more than 40 of the animals. And for campers seeking a unique setting amid the prairies of southwestern Minnesota, Blue Mounds is an inviting natural "speed bump" that rewards those who take the time to slow down and look around.

The campgrounds are situated along Mound Creek at the northern end of the Blue Mounds outcropping. The main campground consists of 73 campsites, laid out along one side of the road or in three main loops on the other. The sites on the outside of each loop are more spacious, and those at the head of the first two loops also face the waters of Mound Creek.

While most of the sites are fairly roomy, the inner campsites are open and therefore might be less appealing. This is also where the RVs and larger camping units tend to park. Each site has the standard state park amenities of a driveway, picnic table, and fire ring with a grate.

The campsites at the head of the loops are very exposed to the rest of the camp and roadway. However, by facing back toward the creek you can at least visually block out others. That's because these loops end at the edge of a small, rocky ridge a few yards above the creek. Simply step back beyond the end of the campsite and you emerge first beneath an oak canopy, then onto a rocky ledge above the water. If this setting sounds appealing, ask for site 11 specifically. To varying

RATINGS

Beauty: ✿ ✿ ✿
Privacy: ✿ ✿
Spaciousness: ✿ ✿ ✿
Quiet: ✿ ✿ ✿
Security: ✿ ✿ ✿
Cleanliness: ✿ ✿ ✿

degrees, the other campsites at these loop heads—12, 13, and 29 through 31—offer similar retreats from the rest of the campground.

Campsites 49 through 59 in the last loop back onto a treed meadow area with grasslands beyond. The top of the third loop is at the end of the roadway into the campgrounds, so more sites line this stretch. Sites 60 through 73 are lined up single-file along this road, with lots of space between them but little privacy.

The 14 remote or walk-in sites are nestled into the woodsy edge in clusters of two and three units to a site. Carts are available at the parking lot located just off the main park road. A central shelter, water source, and toilet provide the only amenities in this area. While not totally private, each site is situated in or at the edge of its own stand of oak trees. Sites 1 through 4 and 5 through 8 are close together but have the woods for partial screening. Sites 13 and 14 are screened from the trail by the shower building. The most private sites are those closest to the lake. These are the sites I'd go after for the most remote and uncrowded experience at Blue Mounds.

Trails passing through this campsite lead out to all the systems in the park—to Upper Mounds Lake and the main campground, and to the Upper and Lower Mound Trail network. The entire park and its trail system are laid out north to south just like Blue Mounds.

The influence of the prairie and forested areas along the creek is reflected in the flora and fauna that abound here. Most striking among the wild plants is the northern variety of cacti that lives in this part of Minnesota. The small prickly pear plants add colorful spots of yellow to the landscape when they blossom in the spring. More evidence of this plant that is so seldom found this far north can be found at the Pipestone National Monument a few miles north of the park.

I camped at Blue Mounds one moonless September night. Coyotes whined in the distance, seemingly waiting their turn to make noise following the cacophony of cries at dusk from the hundreds of blackbirds passing through the park during fall migration.

The strangest sound emanating from the "Mounds" may be the morning "hog call" to the bison

KEY INFORMATION

ADDRESS: RR1, Box 52 Luverne, MN 56156-9610

OPERATED BY: Minnesota DNR, Division of Parks and Recreation

INFORMATION: (507) 283-1307, interpretive center: (507) 283-1310 (May–September)

OPEN: Year-round

SITES: 73 semimodern, 14 walk-in (with carts)

ASSIGNMENT: First come, first served, unless reserved

REGISTRATION: At (866) 85-PARKS (72757); www.stay atmnparks.com

FACILITIES: Restrooms, showers, vault toilets, water

PARKING: At entrance to campground, on each campsite loop; at cart-in camp area

FEES: $7 daily permit, $5 group, $25 annual; camping $15 semimodern, $18 electric, $11 rustic; $8.50 nonrefundable reserve fee

ACTIVITIES: Hiking, swimming, fishing, canoeing, wildflower photography, wildlife viewing

RESTRICTIONS: Pets: Must be on a leash 6 feet or less
Fires: In designated rings only
Alcohol: Not allowed
Vehicles: On designated trails or roads only
Other: Closed to nonregistered campers 10 p.m.–8 a.m.

MAP

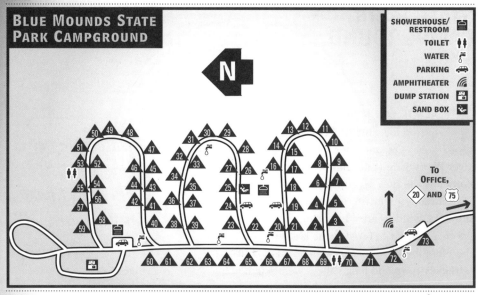

BLUE MOUNDS STATE PARK CAMPGROUND

SHOWERHOUSE/ RESTROOM	
TOILET	
WATER	
PARKING	
AMPHITHEATER	
DUMP STATION	
SAND BOX	

To OFFICE, 20 AND 75

GETTING THERE

Head north from I-90 at the Luverne exit. Continue north through Luverne on US 75 for about 1.5 miles. The first sign on the right directs you to the Interpretive Center; stay straight on US 75 and take the second right to the park entrance at County Road 20 for camping and other amenities.

herd that roams the enclosures built atop the Blue Mounds. The herd keeper gives a high-pitched call out over the prairie meadow announcing the morning feeding. It's quite a sight to see 40 or more bison single-filing it in across the prairie as the sun casts its golden rays on dew drop–covered grasses.

The herd, brought here years ago—transplants from herds in Nebraska and Minnesota (from Mankato's Sibley Park Zoo)—consists of about 20 calf-bearing–aged cows. Calves are born between late April and June. The herd is fed four times daily so your chances of seeing a feeding are pretty good.

There is a small picnic and playground area adjacent to a small swimming area at Upper Mound Lake to round out the amenities at this park. Between the bird-watching, prairie wildflower viewing, and appreciating the geological lay of the land, campers at Blue Mounds will find this part of extreme southwestern Minnesota a "must-visit" site.

GREAT RIVER BLUFFS STATE PARK CAMPGROUND

EVEN IF YOU HAVE miles to go before you need to stop for a night of camping, treat your legs, your eyes, and your spirit to a stop-off at Great River Bluffs State Park—and then plan to camp at one of my favorite sites in the whole state!

Extreme southeastern Minnesota is part of what is called the Driftless area. In geological terms that means this area was not covered in the last series of ice ages. Therefore there are no glacial deposits or drifts. Extremely deep and long valleys were sculpted by melted waters raging through these areas. Today, that unique topography can be experienced firsthand at Great River Bluffs State Park.

Most of the accessible areas of the park are situated along the steep and narrow ridges that fan out like the fingers on a bony hand. One finger has been developed into a modest campsite and another into the group area, while other fingers reach toward the river valley below, offering breathtaking vistas of the mighty Mississippi River just north of LaCrescent.

A red pine corridor, part of a very scenic drive that follows the upper contours of one of many fingers, invites guests to the entrance to the campground. Because the campground lies opposite the entrance to the park, the drive in provides a wonderful opportunity to see what the entire park looks like. The park is adjacent to the Richard J. Doer State Forest, so it boasts its own stately stands of oak and maple as well as graceful forests of red pine. Visitors also enjoy elk corralled in an area just outside the park's entrance.

The campground is a simple loop cut through a stand of oak, maple, birch, and aspen. What's nice about this campground is that the driveways into each site are staggered—you don't see the campsite across the road! Like all looped configurations, those sites on the outside of the loop are more spacious and

> *Breathtaking vistas of the Mississippi Valley in Minnesota's Driftless area will please campers.*

RATINGS

Beauty: ☆ ☆ ☆ ☆ ☆
Privacy: ☆ ☆ ☆ ☆
Spaciousness: ☆ ☆ ☆ ☆
Quiet: ☆ ☆ ☆ ☆
Security: ☆ ☆ ☆ ☆
Cleanliness: ☆ ☆ ☆ ☆

ADDRESS: Park Manager
Great River Bluffs
State Park
Route 4
Winona, MN 55987

OPERATED BY: Minnesota DNR,
Division of Parks
and Recreation

INFORMATION: (507) 643-6849

OPEN: March–October

SITES: 31 semimodern

ASSIGNMENT: First come, first
served, unless
reserved

REGISTRATION: At (866) 85-PARKS
(72757) or online at
www.stayatmn
parks.com

FACILITIES: Restrooms, vault toilets, water

PARKING: At a turnout just
before entering the
campsite loop

FEES: $7 daily permit; $5
group, $25 annual;
camping fee $15
semimodern, $18
electric hookup, $11
rustic; $8.50 nonre-
fundable reservation
fee

ACTIVITIES: Hiking, wildlife viewing, wildflowers,
picnic area

RESTRICTIONS: **Pets:** On leash no
longer than 6 feet
Fires: In designated
fire rings only
Alcohol: Not allowed
Vehicles: On
designated trails or
roads only
Other: Closed to
nonregistered
campers 10 p.m.–
8 a.m.; bicycle camp-
ground nearby; pri-
vate elk ranch with
corral nearby

woodsy because they back up to the forest rather than to other sites. The outer sites tend to be broad rather than deep, but the dense understory of sumac, saplings, and other vegetation screen sites from one another. The sites are shady in summer and brilliantly colored in fall.

A trail curves around the eastern side of the campground and connects at each end with a trail that leads out to an overlook. A small play area for children has been developed at the base of the loop, just inside the campground across from the first site.

This is a long, narrow park with fingers stretching more than 0.5 mile out to overlooks several hundred feet above the Mississippi River. In all, eight separate vantage points overlook this driftless area. There are nearly six miles of trails within the park's boundary. In fall, southeastern hardwoods are in their fiery glory.

The picnic area is off a separate spur, which forks off into two trails each leading to its own overlook.

Native Americans inhabited the area soon after glaciers retreated, and they built mounds along many of the bluffs flanking the river. Settlers turned nearby forests into plowable lands but left the steep slopes alone. In the 1960s reforestation projects began creating plantations of introduced red pine along with native white pine, green ash, and walnut. The park also has a stand of northern white cedar, typically a colder-climate species.

Not all of the park is steep bluffs and deep ravines. There are over 30 patches of prairie, too. Mammals and birds abound. The park is home to a diverse group of animals, including the timber rattlesnakes, six-lined racers (a lizard), and several uncommon bird species, such as the bobolink and Henslow sparrow.

Several miles away, down on the valley floor along US 61, Great River Bluffs State Park offers a five-unit bicycle-camping site virtually on the shoulder of the road. The site is quite modest but there is a tent site with a table and fire ring. Noise from the highway would be intense, but at least you get a reprieve from hectic highway peddling.

MAP

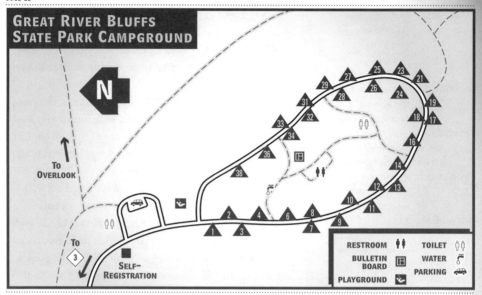

GREAT RIVER BLUFFS STATE PARK CAMPGROUND

N

To OVERLOOK

To 3

SELF-REGISTRATION

RESTROOM	♦♦	TOILET	♀♀
BULLETIN BOARD	⊞	WATER	🚰
PLAYGROUND	🛝	PARKING	🚐

For a small, scenic campground with a unique geological history and spectacular overlooks, Great River Bluffs definitely belongs on the best camping sites list!

GETTING THERE

Take I-90 to the exit for CR 12 (#266) to CR 3 (CR 12 ends at the northern end of the exit ramp). Turn right and follow CR 3 about 1 mile to the park entrance on the right.

HOK-SI-LA CAMPGROUND

> *This enclosed campground is spread beneath lofty cottonwood trees on the banks of the Mississippi River.*

HOK-SI-LA EARNS a place in this book not only for its roomy, spacious campsites but for an unique campground policy. When you drive up to your campsite, you'd better unload all your gear as fast as you can because after 15 minutes you have to remove your car from the campground. Vehicles must be parked outside the security gate during your stay and can only be brought back in on departure. To park your car, hike back to your site—the farthest is about 0.2 miles from the parking lot. Use a cart to haul your camping gear in and out of camp to transport groceries or other items. At Hok-Si-La, it's worth the short trek.

There are four campsite groups at Hok-Si-La; three are for one or two tents, and one area has six designated group sites. The campground is divided into two relatively equal areas. The common central area is composed of a large picnic area, the caretaker's house, and a small complex of buildings: two bathhouses and a dining hall. A chapel, the camp office, and the outer perimeter parking lot take up the rest of the central core. Campsites are clustered on either side of this central hub.

In the northern half of the park is a cluster of 24 campsites. The first cluster, sites A1 through A13 are open, airy, and spacious. Sites A5 through A7 sit at the edge of a large bank that separates the campground from the river. Bottomland trees form a forested buffer between the campers and the water. A trail to the swimming beach leads to the water from a point on the main camp road located just south of A6.

Cluster B, located just beyond cluster A, has three sites, B3, B8, and B9, that overlook Lake Pepin (a widening in the Mississippi River at Lake City). These sites are wooded, shielded by an umbrella of thick-trunked cottonwood trees.

RATINGS

Beauty: ✿ ✿ ✿
Privacy: ✿ ✿ ✿ ✿
Spaciousness: ✿ ✿ ✿
Quiet: ✿ ✿ ✿
Security: ✿ ✿ ✿ ✿ ✿
Cleanliness: ✿ ✿ ✿ ✿

The main campground road bisects the park, creating two areas that run parallel to the lake. Going from cluster units A and B to unit N and the group camps, trekkers walk through groves of spruce and scattered plantings of cedars, red and bur oak, maple, and white pine. The landscape here is very well groomed.

A small cluster of sites, N1, N2, N3, and G0 are off by themselves at the edge of the bank above and back from the lake. The other group camps each have lots of room between them and provide at least three picnic tables, a fire ring, and piped water within a short distance. The sites are large enough to accommodate four or five tents in the center clearing. Sites G4 and G5 are perched on an embankment that drops quickly and sharply to the water.

The N sites are nicely spaced, individual sites that have plenty of room between them. All sites on this side of the grounds are set into small clearings in the thick oak overstory and are very clean and secure. There are several nature trails leading out from this area, including one to Ripple Creek.

The area surrounding Hok-Si-La—Lake Pepin, the lowland forests, and the river bluffs of Wisconsin across the lake—make for magical scenery. A minor downside is the constant buzz of commerce along the river and nearby US 61, a popular scenic drive.

Hok-Si-La campground feels secure and should appeal to both family campers as well as soloists. Lake City, just 2 miles to the south, is the jumping-off point for the big boats on Lake Pepin. A boat ramp is located just outside the park. From here canoeists and kayakers can launch their craft for miles of shore cruising.

KEY INFORMATION

ADDRESS: 2500 North US 61 Lake City, MN 55041

OPERATED BY: City of Lake City

INFORMATION: (651) 345-3855

OPEN: May 1–October 31

SITES: 40 semi-primitive tent sites

ASSIGNMENT: By reservation

REGISTRATION: First night's deposit required (no refunds for cancellation)

FACILITIES: Restrooms, showers, vault toilets, water

PARKING: None at campsites, 15-minute drive-up load/unload; park at entrance to tent-camping area

FEES: $15 regular site, $45 group site; with 3 or more tents, $15 per tent; tent for kids 12 and under or for food, $5 per night

ACTIVITIES: Nature trail, interpretive center, playground, swimming, rockhounding, birdwatching, boating (landing nearby)

RESTRICTIONS: Pets: On leash at all times
Fires: In grills or rings only; no fires on beach
Alcohol: Not allowed
Vehicles: Must park in lot outside campground perimeter
Other: No camping or lifeguard on duty on beach; swim at your own risk; park closed after 10 p.m.; quiet time 10 p.m.– 6 a.m.; no fish in garbage cans

MAP

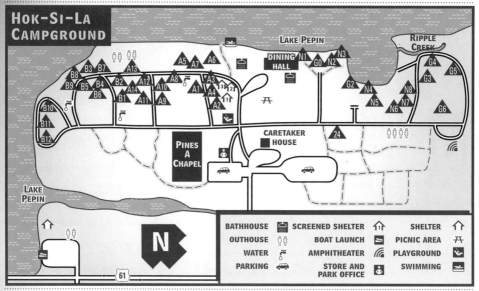

GETTING THERE

From Lake City, go north 2 miles on US 61. The campground entrance is on the right.

MINNEOPA STATE PARK CAMPGROUND

MINNEOPA **S**TATE **P**ARK boasts two distinct highlights: twin waterfalls and the remains of an old gristmill. The waterfalls are the largest falls in southern Minnesota and are cut into soft sandstone, creating a beautiful, deep gorge. Sadly, when I visited this park, a seasonal drought kept the creek bone-dry. Still, the walk through the falls area and the surrounding gorge made the trip enjoyable nonetheless. When the creek is flowing, the falls become a roaring backdrop to several trails that loop through the area providing fantastic overlooks and photo opportunities. This section has a city park feel to it.

The section of the park with the campground is north of the waterfall section, separated from it by MN 68. Each section has its official park entrance. The falls are less than 2 miles from the campground.

The main section of the park follows glacier-carved creek beds created over 15,000 years ago. The creek forming the valley emptied into the Minnesota River. That valley and the gigantic glacial boulders deposited by retreating glaciers in the Ice Age (from bedrock more than 100 miles away) created the prominent features you see in Minneopa Park today.

Sixty-eight campsites are laid out in two crescent-shaped loops that make up the Red Fox Campground. Campsites are set into a mixed forest of silver maples, cedars, and aspen. The first four sites of the A loop are very close to the road. As you follow loop A, the campsites on the outer perimeter are more densely wooded. Each site offers shade courtesy of the full-bodied forest. Sites inside the circle are more confined and thus less private and less spacious. All the sites have the standard-issue fire ring and picnic table. Minneopa does not offer tent pads—just ample flat areas for pitching a tent.

> *Glacier-formed sandstone river terraces and southern Minnesota's largest waterfall add to the charm of this spot.*

RATINGS

Beauty: ☆ ☆ ☆ ☆
Privacy: ☆ ☆ ☆
Spaciousness: ☆ ☆ ☆ ☆
Quiet: ☆ ☆ ☆
Security: ☆ ☆ ☆
Cleanliness: ☆ ☆ ☆ ☆

ADDRESS:	54497 Gadwall Road Mankato, MN 56001
OPERATED BY:	Minnesota DNR, Division of Parks and Recreation
INFORMATION:	(507) 389-5464
OPEN:	Year-round
SITES:	68 semimodern; 6 with electric hookups; group camp
ASSIGNMENT:	First come, first served, unless reserved
REGISTRATION:	At (866) 85-PARKS (72757), or online at www.stayatmn parks.com
FACILITIES:	Restrooms, showers, vault toilets, water
PARKING:	At campsites, visitor center and north entrance to Beaver Creek Valley Trail
FEES:	$7 daily permit, $5 group, $25 annual; camping $15 semimodern, $18 electric hookup, $11 rustic; $8.50 nonrefundable reservation fee
ACTIVITIES:	Hiking, stream fishing, wildlife viewing, natural formations (waterfall, ancient river terraces); historic landmarks
RESTRICTIONS:	**Pets:** On 6-foot maximum leash **Fires:** In designated fire rings only **Alcohol:** Not allowed **Vehicles:** On designated trails or roads **Other:** Closed to nonregistered campers 10 p.m.–8 a.m.

The best sites in loop A are 26 and 28—roomy, private, and under the umbrella of towering oak trees.

Loop B is very similar to loop A except it's a little less shady, having fewer trees. Again, the outside of the loop, especially the higher-numbered sites, offers more room, with the surrounding forested area providing each campsite with a "backyard".

This park is a hiker and biker's holiday in summer and a cross-country skier's delight in winter. The valley is long, flat, and accessible by a gravel road that leads from the campground through more than 2 miles of open prairie strewn with glacial boulders and accented with clumps of sumac, thistle, and scrub cedar. In the fall, wild plum trees are profuse with fruit. This area was heavily grazed by sheep before becoming park property, so the natural reclamation process is still under way.

The historical feature of the park is the Seppman gristmill that sits on a ridgeline overlooking the creek valley. Built in the mid-1860s, the mill saw many prosperous years as it served the areas grain farmers. The double whammy of a damaging lightning strike followed a few years later by a debilitating tornado finally closed the mill as a landmark historical site. The vista from the mill ridge is breathtaking, especially when the valley is awash in fall color.

Minneopa's history includes a time when a local band of Native Americans, called the Tribe of Sixes because they tended to build their dwellings in clusters of six, settled in the area of the park. Later this area was supposed to become a resort, but the Civil War and Dakota Wars of 1862 interfered with its completion.

The oak savannah sections of the park are home to bluebirds, bobolinks, and woodpeckers. Garter and bull snakes are frequent slitherers there, too—both are nonpoisonous.

A beautifully maintained picnic area adjoins the twin waterfall section of this park. A short circuit hike enables visitors to walk along and over the creek in open view of the waterfall. If it has been a dry year, don't expect to see a torrent or even a trickle. However, when the creek is flowing, this should be a spectacular sight—and sound.

MAP

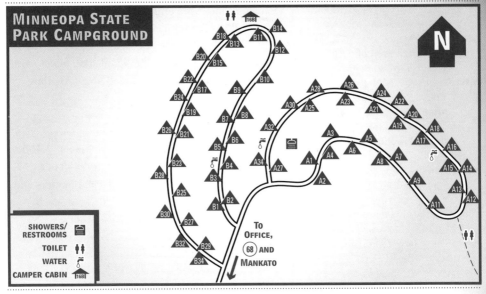

Bring the mountain bikes and cameras, fishing poles and binoculars, and a good pair of hiking shoes—you'll put them all to good use when camping at Minneopa.

GETTING THERE

Go 3 miles west of Mankato on US 169 to MN 68. Go right (west) on MN 68 1.5 miles to the northern park entrance and the campground. To get to the falls, take US 169 right (west) to CR 69 and go west 1.7 miles to the park entrance on the left. Shortcut from the campgrounds to the falls: head back toward Mankato on MN 68, go 0.25 miles and turn right onto Township Road 117. Go south 0.5 miles to the intersection with CR 69 and turn west to the falls entrance, about 0.5 miles on CR 69.

MYRE BIG ISLAND STATE PARK CAMPGROUNDS

> *This island of natural amenities lies on the flat farmland along the Minnesota–Iowa border*

TO HEAR ARCHAEOLOGISTS tell it, it seems no sooner did the last Ice Age retreat from this part of southern Minnesota that the indigenous people began settling around the lakes in this region. After 9,000 years, the Myre Big Island area—now a state park—and the adjoining Albert Lea Lake form a recreational oasis in this otherwise agricultural area so close to the Iowa border.

Campers who enjoy this park can thank Mother Nature for the lakes formed when the ice left and for the other features carved, gouged, and otherwise footprinted in the glacial moraine that gives this area its topography. Those water basins encourage plant growth, and big-woods forests soon flanked the lakes. This, in turn, attracted wildlife.

When humans became motivated by the economics of homesteading and agriculture, many of these areas either disappeared entirely or were severely cut back in area—but at least preserved. This park owes its preservation to amateur archeologist and conservationist Owen Johnson. His efforts in 1947 to create the park have seen the park's area increase tenfold into a nearly 1,600-acre park today.

For campers, this means remnants of oak savannah, northern hardwoods, and wetlands have all be preserved within the boundaries of Myre Big Island State Park. Two campsites, one just inside the park and situated on the western shore of a small inlet on Albert Lea Lake, and one laid out on Big Island offer campers many opportunities to enjoy scores of hiking and biking trails and many more miles of paddle sports out on the lake.

White Fox Campground is the larger of the two grounds with more than 60 sites at the end of a winding gravel road just inside the park. Sites 37 through 50, for all the forests around, look like a large picnic area,

RATINGS

Beauty: ✪ ✪ ✪
Privacy: ✪ ✪
Spaciousness: ✪ ✪
Quiet: ✪ ✪ ✪
Security: ✪ ✪ ✪
Cleanliness: ✪ ✪ ✪ ✪

replete with one fire ring and one shade tree per campsite. Sites 52 and 53 offer a brush buffer between those
sites and are a bit more spacious than previous sites in
this loop. This is a recurring pattern in most state parks—
campsites outside the loop or at the top of the loop tend
to be spacious and more private and can actually border
on natural areas—literally in your tent's backyard.

All the sites in the 60 through 67 grouping are
exposed, not private at all. As the loop continues
around, some understory begins to appear, affording
these campsites some privacy. By the time the loop
returns to the main road, the view from the sites opens
up to the grassy savannah again.

The Big Island Campsite is situated on Big Island
and looks out to the southwest across Albert Lea Lake.
The island is actually a peninsula now, connected to the
mainland by a narrow causeway. Trees are bigger as
you approach the island, with characteristic species
being cottonwoods, maples, and old-growth basswoods.

Campsites are very spacious and cut in to the forest under a spreading canopy of hardwoods. Those situated in the inner loop are shaded by mature maples.
These sites are spacious and look out onto the lake—a
nice bonus because that's where the extra site depth
encourages most RVs to park.

Toward the southern end of the second loop,
where sites 21 through 36 are located, there are sites
that are more wooded, particularly sites 22 and 23,
which back up to the woods and have more overstory
than other sites in the loop. The woods here are typical
of a mature southern Minnesota hardwood forest.
Another preferred group of tent sites is 4 through 7,
which are literally cut back into the woods. Many of
these sites are long and narrow with a modest understory between each one.

The best features of Myre Big Island are the
stands of mature trees (remember, this is in the heart of
flat farm county) and the spattering of wetlands
throughout the prairie areas. These marshy areas are a
showcase of pitcher plants, marsh marigolds, and wild
iris—not to mention a profusion of cattails. There are
several restoration projects under way in the park.

KEY INFORMATION

ADDRESS: Route 3, Box 33
Albert Lea, MN
56007

OPERATED BY: Minnesota DNR,
Division of Parks
and Recreation

INFORMATION: (507) 379-3403

OPEN: Year-round

SITES: 100 semimodern, 4
remote walk-ins

ASSIGNMENT: First come, first
served, unless
reserved

REGISTRATION: Available by calling
(866) 85-PARKS
(72757), or reserve
online at www.stay
atmnparks.com

FACILITIES: Restrooms, showers,
vault toilets, water

PARKING: Backpack parking at
White Fox Camp-
ground, visitor
parking at Big Island
Campground

FEES: $7 daily permit; $5
group, $25 annual;
camping fee $15
semimodern, $18
electric hookup, $11
rustic; $8.50 nonre-
fundable reservation
fee

ACTIVITIES: Fishing, canoeing,
hiking, bird-watch-
ing, wildlife viewing

RESTRICTIONS: Pets: On 6-foot
maximum leash
Fires: In designated
fire rings only
Alcohol: Not allowed
Vehicles: On desig-
nated trails or roads
only
Other: Closed to
nonregistered
campers 10 p.m.–
8 a.m.

MAP

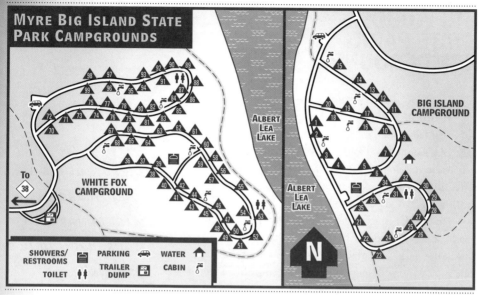

MYRE BIG ISLAND STATE PARK CAMPGROUNDS

WHITE FOX CAMPGROUND

BIG ISLAND CAMPGROUND

ALBERT LEA LAKE

ALBERT LEA LAKE

To 38

SHOWERS/RESTROOMS   PARKING   WATER
TOILET   TRAILER DUMP   CABIN

N

GETTING THERE

Located 3 miles southeast of Albert Lea on CR 38. Take exit #11 (CR 46) from I-35 east to Freeborn CR 38, then turn right (south) to the park entrance straight ahead. Good signage directs one to the park from either I-35 or I-90.

Quiet and patient wildlife viewers will be rewarded with white-tailed deer, raccoon, and even a few bat species. This park is also renowned for being one of the very best bird-viewing areas in southern Minnesota. The list includes American kestrel, great horned owl, American bittern, wood duck, pileated woodpeckers, and the especially graceful white pelican with its six-foot wingspan, which passes through on its fall migration.

There are two large group camps (one's on the island) and several backpacking camping sites in the park accessible from one of the hiking trails in the northern area of the park.

The picnic area has a nice country park setting. Just beyond the picnic area on the northern end of Big Island is a boat launch that gets you out onto the lake, offering miles of shoreline to explore.

Myre Big Island State Park is one of only a very few places to camp in southeastern and south central Minnesota. Its proximity to the main interstate and to Iowa from the south, and its easy access from the Twin Cities, makes it a great campground.

NERSTRAND–BIG WOODS STATE PARK CAMPGROUND

IF YOU ARE DECIDING where to camp to enjoy rich fall colors, look no further than Nerstrand-Big Woods State Park. I love this park, with its rich warm maple reds and golds, the striking glens of brilliant fall colors, and winding, climbing trails underneath a Big Woods canopy.

That said, I must admit that the best campsites in this park are far and few between—in the walk-in section of the park. The main camping area is a typical state park pattern of loop and cut-out campsites. The individual sites are, for the most part, set a fair distance apart but with literally no understory to block views—the entire campground is too open for my taste. However, sites 20, 22, and 23, outside the loop, have more space and privacy and back up to the Big Woods forest.

The campground loop is bisected laterally by a road offering even more spacious, open sites—this is where the RVs herd. It is pretty in the campground, thanks to the towering basswood, red oaks, and maples that make up the mature stand of forest from which the area was developed. A nice trail leads from between sites 18 and 20 to several trail intersections and is less than a half mile from the park's picturesque waterfall.

The very best camping in this park is available at the four walk-in tent sites across from the group site. There's the trade-off: If the group camp is filled with a noisy group, campers across the road are going to suffer. Otherwise the spaciousness of each site and the distance between sites—all of which are nicely screened by dense understory—make these sites worth seeking.

Walk-in distances vary from 12 yards or so to perhaps 40 yards from the parking lot. The sites themselves are at least 40 to 50 yards apart and feature basic amenities such as a fire ring and a picnic table. I camped here late one fall and caution you to keep all your food secure. I had a raccoon snatch a carton of

> *The very best camping sites are at the walk-in campground, with great hiking along trails that lead to a waterfall.*

RATINGS

Beauty: ✯ ✯ ✯
Privacy: ✯ ✯ ✯ ✯
Spaciousness: ✯ ✯ ✯ ✯ ✯
Quiet: ✯ ✯ ✯ ✯
Security: ✯ ✯ ✯
Cleanliness: ✯ ✯ ✯ ✯

KEY INFORMATION

ADDRESS: 9700 170th Street East
Nerstrand, MN
55053

OPERATED BY: Minnesota DNR,
Division of Parks
and Recreation

INFORMATION: (507) 334-8848

OPEN: Year-round

SITES: 51 semimodern, 4
rustic walk-ins

ASSIGNMENT: First come, first
served, unless
reserved

REGISTRATION: At (866) 85-PARKS
(72757), or online at
www.stayatmn
parks.com

FACILITIES: Restroom, showers,
vault toilets, water

PARKING: At the group camping area, 0.3 miles
west of the main
park entrance

FEES: $7 daily permit; $5
group, $25 annual;
camping fee $15
semimodern, $18
electric hookup, $11
rustic; $8.50 nonre-
fundable reservation
fee

ACTIVITIES: Hiking, interpretive
center, picnic area,
volleyball court,
cross-country ski
trails

RESTRICTIONS: Pets: On 6-foot
maximum leash
Fires: In designated
rings only
Alcohol: Not allowed
Vehicles: On desig-
nated trails or roads
Other: Closed to
nonregistered
campers 10 p.m.–
8 a.m.

milk right off the picnic table in the time it took me to retrieve something from my tent, a mere 20 feet away.

Sites 1 and 4 are the farthest from their neighbors, and sites 2 and 3 are fairly close together by walk-in standards. Each campsite backs up to the mature forest of maples and oaks. There is a trailhead at the end of the parking lot that connects to all the routes in the park. At the other end of the lot are trails for snow-shoeing and snowmobiling in winter. There is also a trail that parallels the road to lead campers back to the park's entrance.

There is ample parking (the lot is shared with the group campers), and you'll find water and vault toilets beyond the parking lot.

Regardless of the time of year, Nerstrand-Big Woods offers great trails through stately stands of trees and in some areas along exposed rock that hints at the park's geological history. The forests are all that remain of the more than 5,000 acres of large hard-woods that were common to the area when it was first settled by nonnatives. In fact, it was these insightful homesteaders who realized the value of these forests and managed to secure almost 300 acres of the Big Woods for posterity.

Geologically, the park lies on two horizontal strata laid down by recent glaciation. One layer is glacial drift that is about 150 feet thick and overlies Plattesville limestone (the floor of an Ordovician sea almost 500 million years ago). The upper, more clay-like layer continues to erode, exposing the limestone. There are several places in the park where this extreme erosion is most evident, such as at Hidden Falls, where the creek has slowly but steadily worn away the upper layers, creating shelf 12 feet high by 30 yards wide. Water flowing over this shelf continues to cut into the sublay-ers, constantly digging the pool beneath the falls. Exposed rock along sections of the Prairie Creek bot-toms is yet more evidence of the abrasive action of the water on this layer.

The network of looped trails off the campgrounds can combined to create hikes varying in length and changes in elevation that lead you back to the camp-ground. Fortunately, all these routes intersect very

MAP

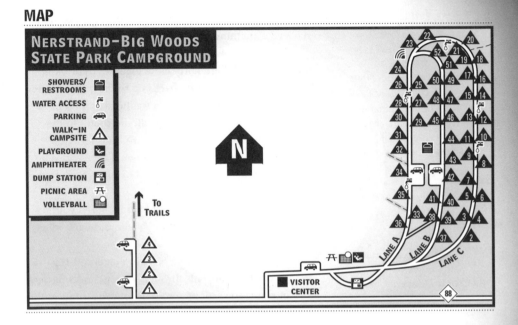

NERSTRAND-BIG WOODS STATE PARK CAMPGROUND

SHOWERS/ RESTROOMS	🚻
WATER ACCESS	🚰
PARKING	🚗
WALK-IN CAMPSITE	⚠
PLAYGROUND	🛝
AMPHITHEATER	🎦
DUMP STATION	🚽
PICNIC AREA	🍽
VOLLEYBALL	🏐

TO TRAILS

N

LANE A
LANE B
LANE C

VISITOR CENTER

88

close to Hidden Falls, so each trail takes you by this geological wonder.

Saving this camping opportunity until autumn may mean a dry creek and no waterfall, but the reds and golds of the forest will more than make up for it.

GETTING THERE

From I-35, take exit #42. At Faribault, go right to CR 20. Turn left (north) on CR 20 and go 6 miles to Cannon City. From Cannon City take a right onto CR 29 (north) and go about 2 miles to the intersection with CR 88. Turn right onto CR 88 and go about 4 miles to the park entrance on the left.

RED PINE FAMILY CAMPGROUND

> *This full-service county park has a 'northern-woods' rustic campsite ideally suited for families with smaller children.*

CLEARY **L**AKE **IS PART** of a regional park system (formerly called Hennepin Parks) that offers a wide range of outdoor activities. The lake has developed trails, some even paved. A beautiful golf course is all the nicer for its clubhouse and an ample picnic area with pavilion. So, why, in the middle of this modern, developed recreational complex would anyone want to camp, especially tent camp?

Cleary Lake actually offers five camping areas: four tightly grouped and confining drive-in campsites and one modest, five-unit site back in the woods just far enough to give a sense of the remote north. Known as Red Pine Family Campground, these five sites are what tent campers are looking for.

Red Pine Family Campground is technically a walk-in camping area. You must park your car at the narrow entrance to the camping area and carry all your gear to your site. However, since the farthest tent site is only about 70 yards from the entrance, it's hardly a trek unless you're lugging a 50-pound cooler. Even with that, though, it's worth the drive to overnight in these spacious tent areas that are cut out of their own section of a large, communal opening in the woods.

The five sites encircle a relatively clear common area, sprinkled with a few oaks, that has a central fire ring. The edges of the clearing stop right at the dense understory that affords ample privacy to each campsite and gives each area its own niche, its own "this is my woods" sensibility. Granted, you can see the other campers from some sites, but it's still better than the clustered, crowded campgrounds of many parks.

The red oaks, green ash, and white pines that dominate the site give a northern lake-country look, even these sites are not near a lake (the south shore of Cleary is about a quarter mile away).

RATINGS

Beauty: ✿ ✿ ✿
Privacy: ✿ ✿ ✿ ✿
Spaciousness: ✿ ✿ ✿ ✿ ✿
Quiet: ✿ ✿ ✿ ✿
Security: ✿ ✿ ✿ ✿ ✿
Cleanliness: ✿ ✿ ✿ ✿ ✿

Speaking of pines, site 5 has an impressive stand of red pines surrounding it. It is the closest campsite to the road but since that lane is not a major traffic thoroughfare, it's hardly noticeable. This is a big site as well: two picnic tables and lots of room. Depending on where you pitch your tent, there's a good chance you won't even see the other sites.

Campsite 1 is the most exposed and looks out, as do all the sites, onto the central clearing. Site 2 is tucked back into a shady area topped with ironwood and ash trees. It's like being in a small glen of shade trees. Site 3 is the most open site, backing up to the woods encircling the campground, but not really tucked into it. There is a trail between sites 3 and 4, although the openness of the clearing makes following this pathway unnecessary for walking around the main camp. Site 4 is also open, yet spacious. Its area for pitching a tent seemed rather steep compared to the other sites. It would be great for drainage but perhaps not ideal for finding a level spot to sleep.

All five sites have a woodsy, lush understory in their backyard. One of the park's pet trails runs behind the campground. This 1.3-mile loop intersects the 3.5-mile trail that follows the entire southern half of Cleary Lake and then meanders through the grassy hills along the northern half of the lake and park.

The only facility at the campsite is the pit toilet at the entrance. Water is available at the communal pump at the Oak Grove group camp: exit the family campground and head toward the lake about 300 yards.

Cleary Lake, at 137 acres, represents about a ninth of the total area of this park. The lake was formed in the glacier moraine deposited during the last Ice Age about 10,000 years ago. The rolling terrain and two creeks that feed into Cleary Lake are typical of the geology of this part of Minnesota. Hiking around the lake is a breeze on the eight-foot-wide paved walk/bike-way that takes a leisurely 1.5 hours to complete. A park road intersects the trail at the extreme southern end of the lake—the same road that leads to the entrance to the Red Pine Family Campground only a few hundred yards to the south.

KEY INFORMATION

ADDRESS:	3000 Xenium Lane N. Plymouth, MN 55441-2661
OPERATED BY:	Three Rivers Park District
INFORMATION:	(952) 447-2171 or www.threerivers parkdistrict.org
OPEN:	May–Mid-October
SITES:	5 rustic tent-only
ASSIGNMENT:	Reservations required, (763) 559-6700
REGISTRATION:	Office open Monday–Friday 8 a.m.–5 p.m., Saturday 8:30 a.m.–12:30 p.m., Sunday noon–4:30 p.m.
FACILITIES:	Table, fire ring, pit toilet; water within short walking distance
PARKING:	To right of entrance
FEES:	$5 daily, $27 annual (second annual car permit is $10 if purchased at with first); camping $10; $7 non-refundable reservation fee
ACTIVITIES:	Swimming, boating, biking, hiking, fishing, golf, play area
RESTRICTIONS:	Pets: On leash on pet trails Fires: In fire rings only Alcohol: Beer and wine permitted Vehicles: Must pay daily or seasonal entrance fee Other: Maximum 6 people per site; no access before 4 p.m.; 14-day maximum stay; quiet hours 10 p.m.–7 a.m.

MAP

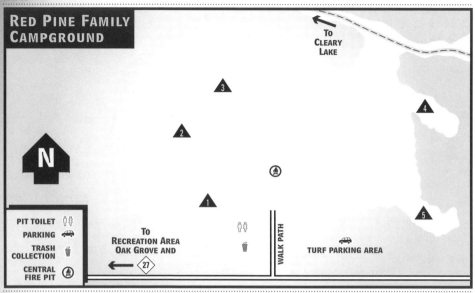

RED PINE FAMILY CAMPGROUND

To CLEARY LAKE

N

3

2

4

1

5

PIT TOILET		
PARKING		
TRASH COLLECTION		
CENTRAL FIRE PIT		

To RECREATION AREA OAK GROVE AND
← 27

WALK PATH

TURF PARKING AREA

GETTING THERE

From I-35 west, south of Minneapolis, take the 185th Street Exit (#84) and go right (west) on CR 60. This turns into CR 21. Continue heading west about 5 miles to CR 27. Turn left (south) to the park entrance on the right.

From US 169 (coming from Shakopee), turn right (south) in Savage on MN 13. Take MN 13 to Prior Lake, CR 21. Turn left (east) to CR 27, then turn right (south) and go to the park entrance on the right.

If you decide to bike or canoe, you can rent these and a few other items right at the park. Fishing is also encouraged.

Red Pine's proximity to the Twin Cities, its county park atmosphere, and the quaint and rustic campsites near Cleary Lake make it a wonderfully close and cozy camping spot especially suited to families with children who want a North Woods experience.

RICE LAKE
STATE PARK
CAMPGROUND

THIS IS ANOTHER state park where the remote, walk-in campsites steal the show from the "semimodern" arrangement developed for the park. These walk-ins are aligned along a gravel road that takes off north from the main campground loop. There are five sites, each with a picnic table and fire pit. There are toilets at the entrance to this area. Water from a hand pump is about one-fifth of a mile at the group site or the same distance back to the regular campground. Unfortunately, they are not very accessible in the winter unless you hike or snowshoe in past the closed gate.

My field notes for this park say "great place to camp" and "private/secluded" in reference to the walk-in sites. These are the kinds of areas where I like to camp. The overstory of oaks and basswood give it a deep-woods feel, and the distance between spacious sites is a real bonus. The walk-in sites are connected to all trail systems and, being on the far end of the campground development, offer immediate access to the undeveloped areas networked by trails throughout the park's eastern half.

The semimodern campground is nestled into tall stands of oaks, basswoods, and maple to give it a solid big-woods feel. There is also a mature understory of younger trees that separates sites and offers some privacy in the two campsite loops.

Loop A has fully wooded sites featuring the basic DNR furnishings of picnic table, fire ring, tent pad, and parking space. Sites are spacious and laid out with ample room to arrande a nice camp area. There is little underbrush between the sites, but the younger trees and saplings that make up the understory provide visual diffusion between one campsite and the next. If the walk-ins are full, loop A, especially those sites on the outer part of the loop, would be a good second choice.

> *A choice remote campsite amid geological and cultural history featuring wonderful seasonal bird-watching*

RATINGS

Beauty: ✿ ✿ ✿
Privacy: ✿ ✿ ✿ ✿
Spaciousness: ✿ ✿ ✿ ✿ ✿
Quiet: ✿ ✿ ✿
Security: ✿ ✿ ✿
Cleanliness: ✿ ✿ ✿

KEY INFORMATION

Loop B is configured similarly to loop A but has a more mature understory. An additional buffer of underbrush blocks direct views into other sites. This is a good thing because the sites in lane B are closer together and less spacious. That being said, loop B seemed to be the lane of choice for larger RVs as well—another reason to consider lane A as a back-up.

Even though there is a "big tree" feel about Rice Lake, it is actually situated in what used to be the southern oak barrens that spread from Iowa all the way up to the Twin Cities. It defined the line between the western prairies and the hardwood forests closer to the Mississippi Valley.

Geologically, this area used to be part of a great sea. Thick bedrock deposited 500 million years ago forms its foundation. The most recent glaciation caused many changes, including large drainage systems from melting ice that worked their way to the even larger cuts made by the prehistoric Mississippi to the east. Rice Lake actually sits on a divide that sent waters east and west. If Rice Lake were drained today, ancient channels carved by that melting ice would be visible on the lake's bottom. Water also played a role in the area's more recent history when local creeks were dammed in attempts to start a water-powered gristmill operation.

Today Rice Lake is a water playground for boaters and fishermen (sorry, no swimming). A remote canoe camp offers five campsites directly across the lake from the park's picnic area.

Astute birders will realize the strategic position of Rice Lake along regional flyways. Its marshes, lake, and meadow provide ideal habitats for protection and rest—not to mention nesting sites for a large number of migrating waterfowl. The mature forests have attracted seven Minnesota species of woodpeckers, including the largest of the lot—the pileated woodpecker (nature trivia: the pileated woodpecker was the inspiration for the famous cartoon character Woody Woodpecker). Look for swans, Canada geese, and a variety of surface-feeding ducks throughout the spring.

If your primary activity while camping is enjoying nature, paddling, or just hanging out away from the congestion, the walk-ins at Rice Lake may be your answer.

MAP

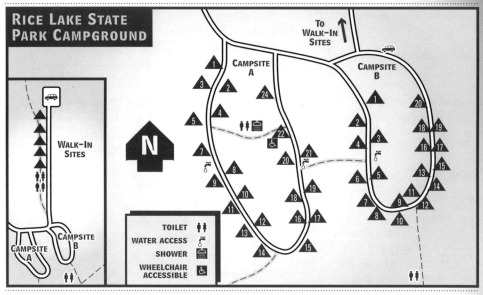

GETTING THERE

From Owatonna, go about 8 miles east on CR 19 for to the park entrance on the right.

SAKATAH LAKE STATE PARK CAMPGROUND

> *Take a tranquil hike over the hills, through lush forests, and along a wide spot in the Cannon River.*

MY INTRODUCTION to Sakatah State Park came while doing research on my last book, a hiking guide for Menasha Ridge Press titled *60 Hikes within 60 Miles of the Twin Cities*. As on the first visit, I was again struck by the lushness of this area along the banks of the Cannon River in southern Minnesota. From a forestry perspective, the Sakatah area delineates a boundary between the Big Woods forest of south-central Minnesota and the oak barrens and savannah areas to the south.

Dense forests of mature oaks in the uplands and cottonwoods in the lower areas provide the overstory for an equally lush array of ground foliage. This lushness helps keep campsites private even in this park of extra-spacious tent sites. The campground is made up of four loops, two on each side of the main campground road. Sites 1 through 15 are laid out in typical DNR fashion: driveway, picnic table, and fire ring. The understory is dense but not as mature as in other areas of the park, yet sites are quiet, and isolated from each other compared to many other campgrounds in the state.

As in most loop configurations, the campsites outside the circle are more spread out. The dense understory is shaded by maples and ash, with sumacs accenting the underbrush. There is a sense of privacy even in this young forest.

Among sites 16 through 33, the outside loop locations are the best choices in the second loop of campsites. These sites, in general, are a bit bigger, and the 10- to 20-yard width of the understory between sites adds to the lushness. The forest of oaks and maples is more mature in this loop.

Bigger still are the sites along the third loop of campsites, numbered 34 through 47. The road through this section has more twists to it, but the bigger sites

RATINGS

Beauty: ✿ ✿ ✿
Privacy: ✿ ✿ ✿ ✿
Spaciousness: ✿ ✿ ✿ ✿ ✿
Quiet: ✿ ✿ ✿ ✿
Security: ✿ ✿ ✿
Cleanliness: ✿ ✿ ✿ ✿

lure RVs in this campground. Still, the tent camper will find sites far enough apart, and the serpentine road winding over the hilly terrain enough to separate these sites from others. Some of these sites have actual tent pads and others ample flat, dry areas for tent pitching. Site 40 is especially nice.

The last loop has quiet and spacious staggered campsites. A hiking trail that cuts between sites 16 and 18 in the second loop (a shortcut to the state trail) leaves the campground again between sites 54 and 56 on its way to the nearby river.

This park provides trails for people on the move. Formed by glacier activity almost 15,000 years ago, the hilly terrain—some more than 400 feet high—is covered with lush stands of oak, basswood, maple, and ash, creating a peaceful wooded retreat at Sakatah. The glaciers also left behind large chunks of ice, some so big that when they melted they created wide lakes in the otherwise narrow river.

Humankind has recorded its history in this park as well. First the Wahpekita of the Dakota Nation inhabited the area and named it Sakatah, which translates into "singing hills." Because of the dense, big woods throughout this area, the Cannon and other rivers became vital water routes for travel between this part of Minnesota and Wisconsin. Trading posts were established, and the Wahpekita developed a village site between the two lakes in the park.

In more recent history, and to the ultimate delight of hikers and bicyclists, the Cannon Valley Company developed a railroad between Faribault and Mankato. Later, as a part of the Chicago and Northwestern Railroad, that portion of the route was abandoned, and the railroad bed was converted into the present-day segment of the Singing Hills State Trail. A Big Woods Loop Trail west of the campground gives hikers a chance to trek through stands of mature hardwoods typical of the Big Woods era of south-central Minnesota.

Ambitious bicyclists can peddle through the forests and grasslands to Faribault, 14 miles to the east or to Mankato, 22 miles to the west.

KEY INFORMATION

ADDRESS: 50499 Sakatah Lake State Park Road Waterville, MN 56096

OPERATED BY: Minnesota DNR, Division of Parks and Recreation

INFORMATION: (507) 362-4438

OPEN: Year-round

SITES: 62 semimodern

ASSIGNMENT: First come, first served, unless reserved

REGISTRATION: At (866) 85-PARKS (72757), or online at www.stayatmn parks.com

FACILITIES: Restroom, showers, vault toilets, water

PARKING: Before entrance to campground, at trailhead to state trail

FEES: $7 daily permit , $5 group, $25 annual; camping $15 semimodern, $18 electric hookup, $11 rustic; $8.50 nonrefundable reservation fee

ACTIVITIES: Hiking, bicycling, snowmobiling on Sakatah Singing Hills Trail, fishing pier, boat ramp, interpretive center
Fires: In designated fire rings only
Alcohol: Not allowed
Vehicles: On designated trails or roads only
Other: Closed to nonregistered campers 10 p.m.– 8 a.m.

MAP

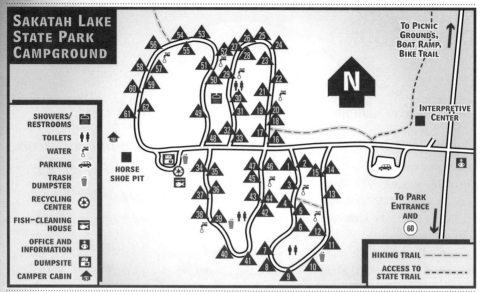

SAKATAH LAKE STATE PARK CAMPGROUND

To Picnic Grounds, Boat Ramp, Bike Trail

N

Interpretive Center

SHOWERS/RESTROOMS	
TOILETS	
WATER	
PARKING	
TRASH DUMPSTER	
RECYCLING CENTER	
FISH-CLEANING HOUSE	
OFFICE AND INFORMATION	
DUMPSITE	
CAMPER CABIN	

HORSE SHOE PIT

To Park Entrance And 60

HIKING TRAIL – – – –

ACCESS TO STATE TRAIL – – – – –

GETTING THERE

The park entrance is on MN 60, 14 miles west of Faribault or 1 mile east of Waterville.

Campers will have many opportunities to view wildlife in the park, particularly at the transitions between dense forest and oak savannah/prairie. Deer, two variety of foxes, raccoons, and muskrats all reside with the park. It's also a wonderful place for bird-watching.

Sakatah Lake can easily keep a family of campers occupied for a weekend or longer depending on the amount of hiking they enjoy. It will be equally pleasant for those who just want to relax under the dense canopy of southern Minnesota's hardwood forest.

SPLIT ROCK CREEK STATE PARK CAMPGROUND

THE AREA AROUND Split Rock Creek is typical of the southwestern area of Minnesota—corn fields and farm country. Split Rock Creek is a quaint oasis of forest and lake smack dab in the middle of this agricultural flatland. The locals use this park for wonderfully relaxing evenings of fishing and hiking alongside the fortunate campers who happen across this spot.

Split Rock Creek is unique in that it is part of a portion of southwestern Minnesota called the Coteau des Prairies—a section of the state whose waters flow not into the Mississippi River but to the west and into the Missouri River. This otherwise insignificant creek flowed uninterrupted through this treeless prairie until 1938, when a dam was built where it flows under County Road 20 today. Since then it has become one of the most popular recreation areas in Pipestone County.

On entering the park, campers may be mildly seduced by the peaceful setting of the lake formed by that dam. The tranquility of the site is further enhanced by the modest forest that spreads from the shoreline. This grove of ash and elm trees was planted nearly 70 years ago by park developers. The road into the campsites follows the western shore of Split Rock Lake toward the short campground loops at the end of the road.

One small but very significant natural attraction of this park, besides the pastoral lake, is the small hill on the left just before you enter the campground loop. Those seemingly insignificant grasses and plants are growing on a hillside that has never seen the blade of a plow and never been scarred by a farmer's furrow. It remains in its original state—a lone remnant of what thousands of square miles of Midwest prairie looked like less than a few centuries ago.

> *A dam built across this tiny creek created one of the biggest recreational getaways in this treeless, grassy expanse of Minnesota.*

RATINGS

Beauty: ✩ ✩ ✩
Privacy: ✩ ✩ ✩
Spaciousness: ✩ ✩ ✩ ✩
Quiet: ✩ ✩ ✩
Security: ✩ ✩ ✩
Cleanliness: ✩ ✩ ✩ ✩ ✩

ADDRESS: 336 50th Avenue
Jasper, MN
56144-9343

OPERATED BY: Minnesota DNR,
Division of Parks
and Recreation

INFORMATION: (507) 348-7908

OPEN: Year-round

SITES: 34 semimodern;
group site

ASSIGNMENT: First come, first
served, unless
reserved

REGISTRATION: Available by calling
(866) 85-PARKS
(72757), or reserve
online at www.stay
atmnparks.com

FACILITIES: Restrooms, showers,
vault toilets, water

PARKING: Parking area along
spur loop across
from sites A–F

FEES: $7 daily permit, $5
group, $25 annual;
camping fee $15
semimodern, $18
electric hookup, $11
rustic; $8.50 nonre-
fundable reservation
fee

ACTIVITIES: Pan fishing in lake,
fishing pier, canoe-
ing, hiking, bird-
watching, swimming

RESTRICTIONS: Pets: Must be on a
leash no longer than
6 feet
Fires: In designated
fire rings only
Alcohol: Not allowed
Vehicles: On
designated trails or
roads only
Other: Closed to
nonregistered
campers 10 p.m.–
8 a.m.

The oblong loop of the campgrounds road offers 28 sites plus a spur loop with 5 more campsites. The first two sites, 2 and 4 on the right, are choice locations for camping near the lake. A basic picnic table, fire ring, and gravel driveway—DNR standard issue—make up the site's amenities. The lake in the background makes these more appealing than those sites laid out in the inner loop. The rest of the sites on the main loop are smallish, keyhole sites fairly close to the road. Those outside the road loop are more spacious and private, albeit having fairly scant understory. The sites at the upper end of the loop (11 through 20) and those inside sites toward the end (21 through 27, the odd-numbered sites) all have electricity, so expect to see the machinery camped at these.

A small looped spur off to the right immediately after site 6 on the right leads to campsites A through F. These are the most private sites, and all are on the lake side of the campground area. Camp here if you can. It's a small enough park that you are still close to all the attractions and amenities, including water and toilets. The road continues beyond these sites and heads to the group camp.

Because Split Rock Creek and Lake are the only large body of water in this grassy sea, it's a natural draw for wildlife, especially waterfowl and other birds. Campers in the spring and fall will witness migrating swans, pelicans, and other winged visitors.

The lake teems with sunfish, walleye, and perch. A trail encircles nearly the entire lake but does not form a loop. Except for a short section at the extreme southern end, hikers can practically circumnavigate Split Rock Lake on foot as well as by water. Bordering the lake along the eastern shore are reeds, and the western edges are forested.

If you are a photographer, you may want to see if the Split Rock Advisory Board is conducting a photo contest.

Pipestone National Monument is only 8.5 miles north of Split Rock Creek. Native Americans would travel to this area from hundreds of miles away to cut the red clay from the earth to make bowls for their peace pipes and other ceremonial items.

MAP

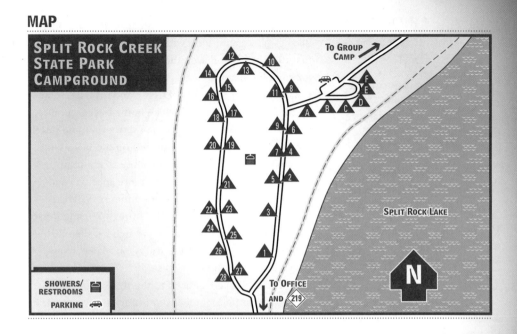

SPLIT ROCK CREEK STATE PARK CAMPGROUND

To Group Camp

Split Rock Lake

N

SHOWERS/ RESTROOMS

PARKING

To Office AND 219

GETTING THERE

From Pipestone, go south about 6 miles on MN 23 to CR 20 in Ihlen. Take CR 20 south about 0.5 miles to the park entrance on the left. From I-90 turn north onto US 75 at Luverne, go approximately 14 miles to CR 2. Turn left (west) and go 5 miles to CR 20 at Ihlen, and then turn left (south) on CR 20 and go about 0.5 miles to the park entrance on the left.

WHITEWATER STATE PARK CAMPGROUNDS

> *This is one of southeastern Minnesota's most popular camping parks—a classic setting rich in resources and scenic beauty.*

DRIVING TOWARD the entrance to Whitewater State Park, particularly from the southern access route on MN 74, one begins to experience the beauty of this area. Dense forests line the valley floors right up to the ridge tops. Occasionally sheer walls of dolomite rock protrude through the canopy of oaks and maples. The winding road, thick woods, and towering rock extrusions all characterize this scenic section of southeastern Minnesota—and are showcased beautifully within Whitewater State Park.

Now the reality check: Expect this park to be very busy between April and Labor Day. It's popularity reminds me of a classic Yogi Berra quote about a very famous and popular restaurant in New York City: "The place is so busy nobody goes there anymore!" It's that kind of skewed rationale that could cause some to think twice about Whitewater—it's always so darn crowded!

That said, there are some options available for persistent campers or those whose appreciation for the amenities, natural and otherwise, can block out the throngs of fellow campers.

The semi-modern campsites, all 106 of them, are configured within five elongated loops in Cedar Hill and Gooseberry Glen campgrounds. Most of the tent camping is at Cedar Hill, with the exception of the four walk-in sites accessible from a road near the trailer sanitation station at Gooseberry Glen.

Sites 1 through 13 are laid out along the floor of the Whitewater River valley in spacious and open sites that offer literally back-to-back camping with little privacy. Sites 14 through 32 have more vegetation and overstory and thus a greater sense of privacy at least. The sites are fairly far apart and roomy, just visually connected.

Sites 33 through 106 are long sites, more open underneath but having large, tall trees above. They are big and spacious—and thus attractive to RVs as well.

RATINGS

Beauty: ✿ ✿ ✿
Privacy: ✿ ✿ ✿
Spaciousness: ✿ ✿ ✿
Quiet: ✿ ✿ ✿
Security: ✿ ✿ ✿
Cleanliness: ✿ ✿ ✿ ✿

Sites 48, and 50 through 75 are smaller spots nestled into slightly taller stands of oak and maple. The pattern for looped campsites plays out here, too—those outside the loop tend to be more private and usually back up to the woods rather than up to another campsite. In fact, sites 62 and 63 back up to the base of a sandstone bluff and have the added luxury of a denser understory of privacy-creating vegetation. An outcropping of sandstone between sites 69 and 70 offers an even more solid sense of privacy between those two sites.

The walk-in sites are toward this bluff line as you move from the larger campground at Cedar Hill toward Gooseberry Glen. A trail off toward the bluff, behind this second campground, provides four walk-in sites with basic amenities. Beyond these sites is the exposed dolomite bluff and the Whitewater River.

Gooseberry Glen tends to collect RVs (perhaps sent there by park officials) because it's a very spacious site with big campsites in an open, grassy area—a picnic area with a grassy parking lot instead of an alluring place to pitch a tent. Still, in a pinch, site 76 is somewhat isolated and private. If you seek shelter from the sun, sites 41 and 42 are particularly shady.

I checked out the primitive group camp across the highway from the main body of the park. Both are big, spacious, and private. They are a good walking distance from most of the park's amenities but worth the price if you truly seek some distance from the city of campers across the road. The capacity of the combined primitive sites is listed as 100 campers, so these are held for organized groups (scouts, church camps, etc.). Still, a camping family reunion could be fantastic if staged here—and the group would be comfortable being isolated.

The reason for this park's popularity is, as stated, the beautiful setting. Couple that with fantastic fishing and a wonderful network of hiking trails, and adventurous campers can find plenty to do here for days on end. The park's geological and cultural history is similar to other parks in the region, having been sculpted by glaciers and receding waters and settled by Native Americans and then early homesteaders. Its lush

KEY INFORMATION

ADDRESS: Route 1, Box 256 Altura, MN 55910

OPERATED BY: Minnesota DNR, Division of Parks and Recreation

INFORMATION: (507) 932-3007

OPEN: Year-round

SITES: 106 semi-modern, 4 walk-ins, primitive group site

ASSIGNMENT: First come, first served, unless reserved

REGISTRATION: At (866) 85-PARKS (72757), or online at www.stayatmn parks.com

FACILITIES: Restrooms, showers, vault toilets, water, fishing pier, amphitheater

PARKING: Next to visitor center and at picnic area; at trailheads throughout park

FEES: $7 daily permit, $5 group, $25 annual; camping $15 semi-modern, $18 electric hookup, $11 rustic; $8.50 nonrefundable reservation fee

ACTIVITIES: Stream fishing for brown and brook trout, hiking, swimming

RESTRICTIONS: Pets: On 6-foot maximum leash Fires: In designated fire rings only Alcohol: Not allowed Vehicles: On designated trails or roads only Other: Closed to nonregistered campers 10 p.m.– 8 a.m.

MAP

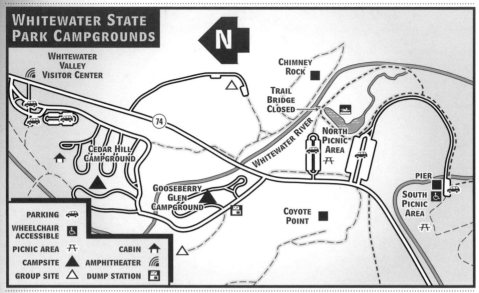

WHITEWATER STATE PARK CAMPGROUNDS

N

Whitewater Valley Visitor Center

Chimney Rock

Trail Bridge Closed

74

Whitewater River

North Picnic Area

Cedar Hill Campground

Gooseberry Glen Campground

Coyote Point

Pier

South Picnic Area

PARKING
WHEELCHAIR ACCESSIBLE
PICNIC AREA   CABIN
CAMPSITE   AMPHITHEATER
GROUP SITE   DUMP STATION

GETTING THERE

From Whitewater, go 1.5 miles north on MN 74 to the intersection with Winona CR 39. Head west on CR 39—it changes to Olmstead CR 2 after about 2 miles. Continue 4 miles on CR 2 to Olmstead CR 10. Turn north and go 3 miles. The Carley State Park entrance is on the left (west).

From Rochester, take US 14 east to St. Charles. From St. Charles, take MN 74 north about 6 miles to the park entrance. From US 61 at Weaver, take MN 74 south. The psark entrance is 3 miles south of Elba on the right.

forests of oak, maple, and basswood; streams full of brown, brook, and rainbow trout; and representative flora and fauna were all treasured by regional conservationists who took action to preserve the area as Whitewater State Park in 1919.

Camping alternative: Here's a camping tip for you to consider. If Whitewater Park is too crowded, consider camping nearby at Carley State Park. It's only about 15 minutes by road from Whitewater and offers 20 campsites in a very pleasant setting of maples, oaks, and pines. There are few amenities besides a short hiking trail, but the peace and quiet may be reward enough. Its proximity to Whitewater's treasure chest of natural attractions makes the short jaunt from campsite to park well worth it.

APPENDIXES **AND** INDEX

POSTSCRIPT

ALTHOUGH **I DID INCLUDE** a few campsites that are officially walk-in sites, none were really that far from the road—a basic criterion for a book featuring drive-up, family camping opportunities. However, these campgrounds, all state parks, are notable for their high-quality sites.

Afton State Park, a few miles southeast of downtown St. Paul, is spread out amid the hills on the western bank of the St. Croix River. The only campground in this park is a mile or two from the parking area, with each campsite laid out in a large pocket of grass on a high, tree-flanked knoll. Great hiking awaits campers here.

Crosby–Manitou State Park is my favorite state park for camping in Minnesota. Rocky high-country North Shore terrain, cascading and sheer-drop waterfalls set the scenery for small, intimate, and minimalist campsites along a trail network. Crosby–Manitou offers near-wilderness camping in fantastic surroundings.

In Frontenac State Park, you'd think such beauty high atop a bluff overlooking the Mississippi at the head of Lake Pepin in southeastern Minnesota would include an equally impressive campground. I wasn't impressed. However, the walk-in sites down and across the road are tucked along the edge of an oak forest bordering a hilly area covered in prairie grasses and sumac. The extra effort you spend finding a cool campsite at one of the walk-ins will be rewarded by great scenery and riverside hikes.

Lake Maria State Park is barely beyond the northermost suburbs of the Twin Cities. It, too, is a great park for hiking but unfortunately does not offer a drive-in campground. Instead it has several sites, each securely nestled in the hardwood forests that cover the area. Each campsite is reached via a spur off the main hiking trail, and each sits beneath maples and oaks. The open understory makes these sites a bit less private than the others mentioned, but the setting and overall charm of this park make it all worthwhile.

APPENDIX A
CAMPING EQUIPMENT CHECKLIST

The basic utensils and smaller items I routinely use on camping trips are conveniently packed in a large storage bin that transfers easily from garage to car in seconds. It makes preparing for a camping trip efficient. All I have to do is grab a tent and sleeping bag, gather food to bring, and away I go. If I don't have it when I get to my campsite, I figure I really didn't need it in the first place. Some of the basic items I do carry are:

COOKING UTENSILS
Biodegradable dish soap
Bottle opener/corkscrew
Coffee pot
Containers of salt, pepper, other favorite
seasonings, cooking oil, sugar
Cups, dishes, bowls
Frying pan (cast iron)
Fuel for campstove
Large water container
Lighter, matches, etc.
Pots with lids (at least two, large and
medium)
Utensils, including big spoon, spatula,
paring knife
Small campstove
Tin foil

FIRST AID KIT
Antibiotic cream
Aspirin
Band-Aids®, assorted sizes
Benadryl®
Gauze pads
Insect repellent
Moleskin®
Personal medications, clearly marked
Sunscreen/lip balm

SLEEPING GEAR
Pillow
Sleeping bag and liner (optional)
Sleeping pad (inflatable or insulated)
Tent with tub floor; tent fly, ground tarp

MISCELLANEOUS
Bath soap (biodegradable)
Camera and film
Camp chair
Candles
Cooler
Deck of cards
Duct tape
Fire starter
Flashlight or headlamp with fresh batteries
Foul-weather clothing
Paper towels
Plastic zip-top bags
Sunglasses
Toilet paper
Water bottle
Wool blanket

OPTIONAL
Barbecue grill
Binoculars (waterproof)
Field guides
Fishing gear
Lantern or tent candles
Maps, charts, other references/information

APPENDIX B
SOURCES OF
INFORMATION

BLACKDUCK RANGER DISTRICT
Tracy Beck, District Ranger
417 Forestry Drive
Blackduck, MN 56630
(218) 835-4291

CHIPPEWA NATIONAL FOREST
HEADQUARTERS
Supervisor's Office
Forest Supervisor: Norm Wagoner
200 Ash Avenue NW
Cass Lake, MN 56633
(218) 335-8600; (218) 335-8632 (TTY)

DEER RIVER RANGER DISTRICT
Wade Spang , District Ranger:
1037 Division Street
Deer River, MN 56636
(218) 246-2123

GUNFLINT RANGER DISTRICT
Dennis Neitzke, District Ranger
2020 West MN 61
Grand Marais, MN 55604
(218) 387-1750 voice and TTY
gunflint@fs.fed.us

ISABELLA WORK STATION
9420 MN 1
Isabella, MN 55607
(218) 323-7722

KAWISHIWI RANGER DISTRICT
Mark Van Every, District Ranger
118 South Fourth Avenue East
Ely, MN 55731
(218) 365-7600; (218) 365-7602 (TTY)
kawishiwi@fs.fed.us

LACROIX RANGER DISTRICT
Constance Chaney, District Ranger
320 North MN 53
Cook, MN 55723
(218) 666-0020 (voice and TTY)
lacroix@fs.fed.us

LAURENTIAN RANGER DISTRICT
Allan Bier, District Ranger
318 Forestry Road
Aurora, MN 55705
(218) 229-8800 voice and TTY
laurentian@fs.fed.us

MARCELL RANGER DISTRICT
Wade Spang, District Ranger
49554 MN 38
Marcell, MN 56657
(218) 832-3161

APPENDIX B
SOURCES OF
INFORMATION
(continued)

MINNESOTA STATE PARKS/STATE FORESTS
Department of Natural Resources
500 Lafayette Road
St. Paul, MN 55155-4031
(651) 296-6157
(888) MINNDNR
Reservations: (866) 85PARKS or
www.stayatmnparks.com
www.dnr.state.mn.us
info@dnr.state.mn.us

SUPERIOR NATIONAL FOREST
Forest Supervisor's Office
Jim Sanders, Forest Supervisor
8901 Grand Avenue Place
Duluth, MN 55808
(218) 626-4300; (218) 626-4399 (TTY)
r9_superior_NF@fs.fed.us

TOFTE RANGER DISTRICT
Jackie Andrew, District Ranger
P.O. Box 2159
Tofte, MN 55615
(218) 663-7280 (voice and TTY)
tofte@fs.fed.us

WALKER RANGER DISTRICT
Tom Somrak, District Ranger:
201 Minnesota Avenue East
Walker, MN 56484
(218) 547-1044

INDEX

ABOUT THE AUTHOR

TOM WATSON GREW UP camping in Minnesota, first as an Eagle Scout with Troop 22 in Minneapolis, and later as a college student studying Forest Resource Management at the University of Minnesota, and then throughout his life in various professions, including as a freelance writer specializing in outdoor subjects.

Tom is an avid sea kayaker, naturalist, freelance writer, and photographer who has spent 30 years enjoying Minnesota's outdoor treasures. This is Tom's second book for Menasha Ridge, following his *60 Hikes within 60 Miles of the Twin Cities,* released in 2002.